Dear Christine,
Warm wishes,
Kevin

Memory & Injustice

Wrongful Accusations in the United Kingdom

memoryandinjustice.co.uk

Edited by Kevin Felstead

Copyright © 2024 Kevin Felstead

All rights reserved. This book or any portion thereof may not be reproduced or used in any means whatsoever without the prior written permission of the author except for the use of brief quotations in a book review.

ISBN-13: 979-8-8731-1157-2

DEDICATION

This book is dedicated to Janet and Michael.

CONTENTS

Acknowledgements	i
Preface	iii
Introduction	vii
Part One	
The return of the repressed	1
The British False Memory Society	21
Two case studies	41
Part Two	
Creating nightmares	58
The Carol Felstead scandal	75
2015 Inquest	105
Part Three	
The BFMS 2014 – 2023	140
Renewed media interest	148
Creating Hysteria: Carl Beech	152
2023 – Two cases studies	159
The caseload of the British False Memory Society	175
References	198
Conclusion	201
Afterword	205

ACKNOWLEDGEMENTS

Front cover with kind permission by Peter Brookes and the *Times* Newspaper.

Andy Malkinson whose conviction was quashed in the Criminal Court of Appeal in 2023 after serving a 17-year prison sentence for a crime he didn't commit.

I would like to thank the contributors to this book: Claire Anderson, Solicitor; Professor Christopher French; Professor Henry Otgaar; Dr Lawrence Patihis; Dr Michael Naughton, who have kindly taken time out from their busy schedules to contribute to this project.

Thanks to Deborah and Michael (names have been changed) for sharing information and allowing me to write up your case study.

To Linda and Ronald who made an indelible impression. I remember your trial as if it were yesterday.

Special thanks to Mark Pendergrast who kindly gave permission for me to re-publish chapter one – 'The Return of the Repressed' from his magisterial book, *Memory Warp – How the Myth of Repressed Memory Arose and Refuses to Die* (Upper Access Books, Hinesburg, Vermont, 2017).

With thanks to my proof-readers who read early draft chapters of the manuscript: Lisa, Madeline, Raphael, and Simon.

A big thank you to Raph for help and support with graphics

and other technical issues. I would never have got over the line without your pragmatic input.

Thanks to my former colleagues and members of the BFMS for your support and friendship over the last decade.

Last but certainly not least, love and warmest thanks to my wife, Maria, who, in addition to reading draft chapters and commenting on a draft manuscript, has supported me and provided critical advice throughout not only *this* project, but with my family's personal encounter with our broken justice system over the last 19 years.

PREFACE

By Claire Anderson

Many years ago, in my capacity as an experienced criminal defence lawyer, I attended a lecture arranged by the British False Memory Society (BFMS) about how so called 'false memories' could be created.

The speaker was an eminent American psychologist and memory expert who took her audience through research and the methods of implanting false memories into an individual's mind.

She showed us how a childhood photograph could be digitally altered, in one case to show the relevant child with a bandaged head. The photograph was then shown to the now adult subject of the photograph, who was encouraged to recall the trauma of sustaining the head injury which they were told was caused after a fall from a tree.

With a little coaxing, the subject of the experiment was able to recall in considerable detail, the phantom accident, even remembering a non-existent hospital visit and the get-well gifts they received from family and friends.

I was absolutely fascinated by this, and there began my career-long interest in false memory and my long association with the BFMS.

I have been practicing criminal law, specialising in representing those accused of sexual offences, for over 30 years. Allegations of a sexual nature fall into a very different category to the vast majority of other criminal allegations.

There has always been, and there remains an enormous stigma that often attaches to those accused of such horrible crimes. Even an arrest, which does not lead to charges, can cause the accused party to lose their employment and they also sometimes face being alienated by family and friends. Unfortunately, there is still a large section of society that believes there is 'no smoke without fire,' which I am sure any party cleared of committing a sexual offence, will unhappily tell you.

False memory cases are in yet another category. They are always historic, and often involve an accuser who has previously enjoyed a very happy and stable relationship with the party accused.

In my experience of these cases, there is often a similar thread that runs through them all. A child enters teenage years and then adulthood but struggles to find their feet in an ever-challenging world. They are supported and encouraged, often by the accused person, to seek therapy to help address their growing anxieties. The therapy sessions happen and then something shifts. The accuser becomes withdrawn and distant until one day, to the shock and horror of the accused, the accuser recounts incidents of childhood abuse which have apparently been repressed for a lifetime and only now recovered through therapy with a (possibly controversial) therapist.

I do of course share the well-established view of the BFMS, that sexual abuse is an abhorrent act. It destroys lives and perpetrators must be brought to justice and suitably punished. It is however important to stress that sometimes a fragile mind can be encouraged to develop a 'memory' that has been implanted, and not recovered, and it is those accused in these cases that have turned to the BFMS over their 30-year history where they have received immeasurable support and guidance from the incredible team. Regular newsletters and annual conferences have allowed BFMS members to share their stories of devastation and fractured families and often the loss of relationships with those dearest to them. It is truly heartbreaking.

It has been my absolute privilege to provide legal representation and support to many clients referred to me by the BFMS over the years and I have huge admiration and respect for Dr Kevin Felstead, Madeline Greenhalgh and all the other individuals dedicated to helping those falsely accused.

Kevin Felstead's book is a fascinating and enlightening read which takes the reader though the power and danger of false memory and is a salutary reminder that in life, everything is not always quite as it seems.

Claire Anderson – Criminal Defence Lawyer.

INTRODUCTION

By Professor Chris French

Twenty years ago, I accepted an invitation to join the Scientific and Professional Advisory Board of the British False Memory Society (BFMS). I was more than happy to accept that invitation. By that point, the BFMS had already been in operation for a decade. It was founded in response to the large number of cases in the UK at that time involving accusations of childhood sexual abuse (CSA) based upon nothing more than apparent 'memories' of such abuse that had been 'recovered' during therapy for a wide range of common psychological problems such as depression, anxiety, eating disorders, low self-esteem, and so on. Prior to entering therapy, the accusers in such cases had no such memories.

The obvious worry in this situation was that those apparent memories were not, in fact, based upon events that had actually taken place in objective reality but were false memories, unintentionally produced by the therapy itself. Today, we can be absolutely certain that inappropriate forms of therapy do indeed have the potential to generate such false memories, often with devastating consequences. Memories of a normal, happy childhood are replaced by nightmarish memories of horrific abuse. Families are torn apart. From the start, the BFMS provided desperately needed emotional support and legal advice to those accused.

The idea that traumatic memories are repressed is a cornerstone of psychoanalytic theory. It is claimed that once such memories are repressed, they become totally inaccessible to consciousness. Repression is held to be an automatic defence mechanism that is completely beyond voluntary control. According to psychoanalytic theory, even though these memories are no longer accessible to consciousness they can still be the root cause of a wide range of serious psychopathological conditions. Repressed memories, it is said, can sometimes re-emerge spontaneously into consciousness but more likely it will require the application of a range of so-called memory recovery techniques by a skilled psychotherapist for this to happen. These techniques include hypnotic regression and guided imagery. What is more, it is claimed that it is essential that these traumatic memories are recovered and 'worked through' if there is to be any hope of recovery. The truth is, however, that most scientific memory researchers are extremely dubious about the very existence of repression.

My own interest in the topic of false memories had its origins in my general interest in the psychology of ostensibly paranormal experiences. The techniques used in attempts to 'recover' memories of alien abduction or of past lives are exactly the same techniques as those used by therapists to 'recover' memories of presumed childhood abuse – even in clients who initially strongly deny that any such abuse ever took place. It is easy to see why most people find it easier to believe that memories of being abducted by aliens or of a past life as Mary Queen of Scots are false memories as compared to 'recovered' memories of being the victim of CSA. For one thing, it is now acknowledged that CSA is much more widespread within society than was once recognised and that it can sometimes cause devastating psychological damage. Secondly, most people are not aware that psychoanalytic ideas have generally been rejected by scientists and psychoanalytic theory is viewed as nothing more than pseudoscience. It must follow, however, that if one would be extremely sceptical of claims of alien abduction or past lives based upon the application of dubious 'memory recovery' techniques, one should logically apply the same scepticism to claims of alleged CSA obtained using the same techniques if there is no independent evidence to support them.

In this book, Kevin Felstead provides a detailed history of the formation and development of the BFMS but he has done much more besides. The case histories contained within these pages, including that of Kevin's own sister, provide powerful insights into the pain and suffering that misguided belief in the concept of repression can cause. I am proud to have played a small part in supporting the work of the BFMS in its attempts to at least mitigate the damage done.

Professor Cristopher French is Emeritus Professor and Head of the Anomalistic Psychology Research Unit at Goldsmiths University.

PART ONE

This chapter was originally published in Mark Pendergrast, *Memory Warp* (Upper Access Books, Hinesburg, Vermont, 2017). This (slightly) edited version is reprinted here by kind permission of the author.

The Return of the Repressed

IT HAS BEEN OVER TWO decades since I wrote *Victims of Memory*, an exploration of the debate over the accuracy of so-called repressed or recovered memories. In his book review in *Scientific American*, Daniel Schacter, the Harvard psychology professor, whose work on memory helped to inform my own, called *Victims of Memory* "an impressive display of scholarship, a comprehensive treatment of the recovered-memories controversy." Now it is time to revisit and up-date this extraordinary phenomenon. Although "repressed memories" have been widely discredited among those who study the science of memory, there appears to be a resurgence of belief in this dangerous theory. Consequently, I have updated my research on the subject. The book you hold in your hands is partly a social and cultural history of our recent past, documenting how this incredible juggernaut of pseudoscience and malpractice, which caused so much harm, came to be. But it also shows how these misguided theories continue to fester. They will inevitably cause another major outbreak and damage the lives of additional millions of people if we do not learn from the past. Rather than calling it a new edition, I have given it a title to indicate the drama and urgency of the subject: *Memory Warp: How the Myth of Repressed Memory Arose and Refuses to Die.*

The first edition of *Victims of Memory* was published in 1995 at the height of the epidemic of false memories of childhood sexual abuse, fomented by a mistaken, pseudoscientific form of psychotherapy. The theory behind this fad stemmed from Sigmund Freud's work a century beforehand, in the 1890s. He called it his "seduction theory," which he himself soon abandoned. But the idea – that people can "repress" or "dissociate" years of traumatic childhood memories and then recall them as adults – refused to die, in part because it provides an appealing plot device for novels, movies, and sensational media coverage, and because many psychologists have imbibed the theory somewhat like mother's milk. It has become an underlying professional assumption that people really can and do banish traumatic memories from their consciousness. And Freud himself promulgated his modified theory as "the return of the repressed" – the pseudoscientific notion that buried desires or fears return in symbolic dreams or actions.

Freud's theory was resurrected in the 1980s by a group of self-described feminist therapists who were concerned about sexual abuse and who believed that women with "symptoms" such as depression, eating disorders, or sexual issues must have been molested as children and repressed the memories so that they had no current knowledge of a horrific childhood. Only by remembering the abuse – often incest – would they be healed. These therapists believed that they could help their clients unearth these repressed memories through methods such as hypnosis, dream analysis, interpretation of bodily pangs, induced panic attacks, or group experiences. In 1988, with the publication of *The Courage to Heal*, by Ellen Bass and Laura Davies, this movement exploded into a fully-fledged epidemic in which women in therapy became convinced that they should accuse their fathers of having raped them for years during their childhood and, with the encouragement of their therapists, they cut off all contact with their families. "Before" and "after" therapy letters such as these became all too common.

May 1987

Dear Dad,

Just a note to thank you for taking such good care of me and my friend during our much-too-short stay. My friend is impressed and a bit envious of the loving relationship and open lines of communication which you and I share. I love you and I'm glad you're my dad!

Love D

November 1989

I am writing this letter for two reasons: (i) to attain closure for myself regarding my relationship with you and (ii) in the hope that you will seek help before you hurt anyone else the way you hurt me. I have spent 37 years of my life denying and minimizing the torture that was my childhood and adolescence. I genuinely hope this letter causes you to seek help – you are a very sick man. I do not wish to hear from you unless you are willing to admit the things you did to me and to seek help for your sickness.

It was ironic that "feminist" therapists were the avatars of this destructive phenomenon. One retractor (someone who later realized she had developed false memories due to misguided therapy) wrote poignantly about her own recovered-memory experience, in which she became convinced that she had so-called multiple personality disorder. "It robs women of all power and control over themselves. If I really hated women and wanted to keep them in a completely powerless and childlike state, the best way to do that would be to remove their faith and trust in their own minds and make them dependent." That is precisely what happened in this form of "therapy," which frequently managed, quite literally, to turn women into helpless, suicidal children clutching their teddy bears and shrieking in imagined pain and horror. The repressed memory-hunt breathed new life into one of the most damaging and sexist traditions in our culture – the subtle message to women that they can gain power and attention primarily through the "victim" role.

It is difficult to convey how saturated our culture became with the repressed memory phenomenon. In her 2010 memoir, *My Lie*, retractor Meredith Maran described her quest to recall how her father must have abused her. "I drove back across San Francisco Bay (in 1989), back to Planet Incest, where the question was always incest and the explanation was always incest, and no one ever asked, are you sure?"

Many hundreds of lawsuits were filed by therapy patients with brand new abuse "memories." Thousands of stunned parents became the first innocent people targeted by the repressed memory epidemic. In 1992 the National Organization for Women published *The Legal Resource Kit on Incest and Child Sexual Abuse*, noting that many adult victims had no idea what had happened to them until they entered therapy. "Civil legal remedies are crucial to deter these acts." In the 1990s over 500 reported cases were filed in which the only evidence stemmed from recovered memories – 15 percent were criminal, 85 percent civil cases. Hundreds of additional cases were quietly settled without formal filings, as many parents were embarrassed, devastated, and terrified, or they wished to avoid a lawsuit against an obviously mentally ill daughter.

In their landmark 2015 book, *Mistakes Were Made (but not by me)*, social psychologists Carol Tavris and Elliot Aronson offered a succinct summary of the absurdities of the repressed memory epidemic:

Under hypnosis, they said, their therapists enabled them to remember the horrifying experiences they had suffered as toddlers, as infants in the crib, and sometimes even in previous lives. One woman recalled that her mother put spiders in her vagina. Another said her father had molested her from the ages of five to twenty-three, and even raped her just days before her wedding – memories she repressed until therapy. Others said they had been burned, although their bodies bore no scars. Some said they had been impregnated and forced to have abortions, although their bodies showed no evidence. Those who went to court to sue their alleged perpetrators were able to call on expert witnesses, many with impressive credentials in clinical psychology and psychiatry, who testified that these recovered memories were valid evidence of abuse.

As families were torn asunder by such recovered memory allegations, in 1992 Pamela and Peter Freyd founded the False Memory Syndrome Foundation, recruiting a stellar board of scientific advisers such as Elizabeth Loftus, Martin Orne, and Paul McHugh. The FMS Foundation began to educate psychologists, the media, and the general public about suggestive therapy based on the unproven theory of massive repression. In return the true believers in repressed memory called the FMS Foundation a group of perpetrators in denial, rather than anguished parents who had lost their children to a delusion.

Members of the British False Memory Society, founded in 1993, were equally vilified, American psychiatric fads, and social concerns spread with astonishing rapidity throughout the English-speaking world. There is a paradoxical historic symmetry involved here. Near the end of the two-century-long European witch craze, the Puritans imported witch-hunting to North America. As a result, in 1692, twenty innocent people were put to death in Salem, Massachusetts. Three hundred years later, Americans returned the favour by exporting the paranoid search for mythical Satanic ritual abuse cults, repressed incest memories, and child sex rings.

As this book documents, the American virus was carried by "experts" who ventured across the Atlantic to share their views with British colleagues. More than that, however, the ground was prepared by the printed word. Not since *The Malleus Maleficarum* was published a few years after Gutenberg's invention, have we seen such evidence of the power of books to affect lives. *The Courage to Heal* spread the gospel of recovered memory and spawned many imitators.

As the epidemic of illusory abuse memories was more widely recognized in the mid-1990s, many professional associations issued cautionary statements, such as this 1994 conclusion from the American Medical Association: "The AMA considers recovered memories of childhood sexual abuse to be of uncertain authenticity, which should be subject to external verification." As a consequence of scientific books and articles by psychologists, sociologists, and critical thinkers such as

Elizabeth Loftus, Richard Ofshe, Carol Tavris, Richard McNally, Paul McHugh, Harrison Pope Jr, Frederick Crews, John Kihlstrom, Paul Simpson, Elaine Showalter, and others, the public began to realize there were serious, controversial issues involved with recovered memory therapy and diagnoses of multiple personality disorder (MPD).

Given the powerful ideological and political movement pushing the epidemic, and the enormous financial rewards involved in turning a depressed housewife into an MPD patient needing years of hospitalizations, scientific information and academic debates were insufficient to halt the burgeoning international epidemic of false memories. Instead, in the late 1990s, million-dollar lawsuits against therapists, brought by women whose lives and families had been nearly destroyed by the misguided therapy, caused a decline in the overt practice of repressed memory therapy, and resulted in the closing of most dissociative disorder clinics in which alleged MPD patients had been held in a modern version of mental health snake pits. These lawsuits were mounted by lawyer-psychologist Christopher R. Barden, who used a multidisciplinary approach of litigation, prosecution, regulation (licensing revocations), education of the public through the media, and proposed legislation. Barden hammered home the point that such controversial, potentially harmful forms of psychotherapy were egregious examples of consumer fraud and the lack of informed consent. As a result, the epidemic was widely criticized and publicized by the turn of the century, and repressed memories were no longer admissible (when so identified) in most courtrooms.

As Harvard psychology professor Richard McNally observed in 2005, "The notion that traumatic events can be repressed and later recovered is the most pernicious bit of folklore ever to infect psychology and psychiatry. It has provided the theoretical basis for 'recovered memory therapy' – the worst catastrophe to befall the mental health field since the lobotomy era."

Most reputable memory scientists agree with that assessment. "There is no good scientific evidence that these unconscious forces exist," wrote psychologist Charles Fernyhough in *Pieces of Light*, his 2012 book on memory. "Traumas are remembered, and they are remembered only too painfully. They may not be thought about for a long time but they are not forgotten."

In *Victims of Memory*, I included four chapters of verbatim interviews – with therapists, "Survivors," the accused, and retractors – conducted in the early 1990s at the height of the repressed memory epidemic. These interviews, available in the book, *The Repressed Memory Epidemic* (Springer, 2017), and on my website, www.markpendergrast.com, offer compelling evidence that many psychotherapists were invested in belief in repressed memories of sexual abuse, and that they had helped clients (mostly women) to recall mythical abuse. The interviews documented the human devastation that resulted.

It was a terrible phenomenon, and I am proud that my book, along with many other books, articles, and lawsuits, helped to alert the public, professionals, and the courts to the perils of the repressed memory epidemic. I have written many other books about an array of topics, the histories of coffee, Coca-Cola, disease, detectives, and mirrors, among others – that have taken me all over the world. But *Victims of Memory* has been my most important work. I certainly don't want this to come off as braggadocio, but when someone tells you, "Reading your book saved my life. I was going to kill myself," it means so much. Or emails out of the blue such as this one: "After realizing my 'recovered memories' acquired during my 'therapy' were delusions, your book gave me the confidence to pursue my lawsuit and psychology board complaint."

It was also in writing about this issue that I became a real science writer. I realized that the scientific enterprise was not simply a dry intellectual pursuit. It demands hypotheses that can be proved or disproved, encourages the use of control groups, requires studies that replicate results. Scientists are not immune to error, by any means, but when they have overreached and drawn wrong or fraudulent conclusions – as with cold fusion, perpetual motion machines, phrenology, or thalidomide – further exploration and experimentation eventually provide correctives. But repressed memory is pure pseudoscience, a matter of faith rather than anything that can be proved or disproved. I came to realize that science and accompanying informed consent can save sanity and lives.

Nonetheless, despite the furore over false memories produced by pseudo-scientific theories, those who believed in recovered-memory therapy did not give up their belief system – and that includes not only those in the United States, but in Canada, the United Kingdom and other English-speaking countries, the Netherlands, and elsewhere. The repressed memory epidemic spread like a pandemic wave. Thus, in 2002, when I spent two months working in Bradford-on-Avon for the British False Memory Society, I found that the belief in repressed memories, multiple personalities, and Satanic ritual abuse cults was thriving there. I concluded that the UK lagged the USA by a few years but had learned from Americans all too well.

Kevin Felstead, the communications director of the British False Memory Society, wrote on March 30, 2017, "We have taken eight new cases in March alone, including another tragic case yesterday. We were involved in two separate Crown Court trials in January." Far from winding down, the BFMS is, unfortunately, busier than ever.

Indeed, the sex abuse hysteria virus cross-pollinated from multiple directions, not just from the United States. For instance, New Zealand therapist James Bennett ventured to England in 1986 to indoctrinate disciples in his disturbing version of recovered memory called "primary activation." Rosemary Crossley's "facilitated communication," a kind of human Ouija board using severely handicapped children, was exported from Australia to the United States in 1989, resulting in many false accusations of sexual abuse. Swiss psychologist Alice Miller was a formative influence in the recovered memory movement. And Czech Stanislav Grof took his "holotropic breathwork" – a form of hyperventilation often leading to "memories", along with violent shaking, gagging, vomiting, and speaking in tongues – to the USA in 1967, but it also found its way, along with other alarming techniques, to the Findhorn Foundation in Scotland.

In other words, no one should get too smug about "those crazy Americans." Instead, we should examine how human beings – wherever they may live – can come to believe in destructive untruths. How can well-intentioned people cause such grievous harm? How can the past be re-written with such ease? These are questions that transcend national borders.

During the summer of 1995, I ventured to England to conduct interviews with British recovered memory therapists, Survivors, accused parents, and retractors. The stories I heard were, unfortunately, all too familiar to me. When I took taxis in London, I learned that the cabbies had to pass a stringent series of tests before they were certified as possessing "The Knowledge." It struck me as ironic that British taxi drivers were better trained than British psychotherapists. If you wanted to get from Victoria to Strand, you were in capable hands. But *caveat emptor* to anyone who opened his or her vulnerable mind to a psychotherapist untutored in the science of human memory.

Rather than facing the overwhelming evidence that a sizable number of their profession violated the Hippocratic oath – "First do no harm" – the professional associations reacted to the controversy mostly by looking the other way, while trying decorously to cover their behinds. They preferred to sweep this embarrassing epidemic under the rug, dismissing it as the work of a few fringe therapists, while still maintaining that the theory of repressed memory has validity. As psychologist Richard Noll observed, they would rather "move on silently and feign forgetfulness."

Thus, repressed memories did not disappear. Indeed, the idea that people could completely forget years of childhood sexual abuse and then remember the abuse later has become enshrined in the popular imagination, despite its widespread scientific debunking.

Once an idea enters the cultural mainstream, it has a way of resurfacing like a bloated corpse every few years. The corpse has risen again if it ever truly sank. As the 21st century dawned, repressed memories began to come back into style with the mounting hysteria over accusations of sexual abuse by priests. While most of the priest cases involved always-remembered abuse that was all too real, a subset, such as the case that sent Paul Shanley to prison in 2002, were encouraged through repressed memory therapy. In 2015, sociologists Carol Tavris and Elliot Aronson observed, "While the (repressed memory and day-care sex abuse hysteria) epidemics have subsided, the assumptions that ignited them remain embedded in popular culture." They were correct that the underlying assumptions remain. Unfortunately, the repressed memory epidemic has not really "subsided." While it was slowed by scientific analysis and retractor lawsuits, the epidemic continues to this day.

Since the height of the repressed memory epidemic, media coverage has swung wildly between solid scientific reports on the malleability of memory to uncritical regurgitation of recovered memory claims. Most young journalists don't know what happened during the "Memory Wars" decade that followed the 1988 publication of *The Courage to Heal* and similar books. Add to that the impact of the Internet and acceptance of fake news and conspiracy theory as reality, and you have a recipe for disaster.

It is an indication of our culture's continuing credulity and fascination with allegedly hidden sexual abuse that a fake news story in late 2016 alleged that Comet Ping Pong, a pizza restaurant in northwest Washington, was harbouring young children as sex slaves as part of a child-abuse ring led by Hillary Clinton. A 28-year-old father went to the restaurant and opened fire with his assault rifle. Luckily, no one was hurt. We have not learned sufficiently from the past, and we could be condemning ourselves to repeat it. But we may call it by another name, undoubtedly a more pleasant-sounding one.

Or maybe our culture won't need to rename it. Just as the book was about to go to press in 2017, Netflix aired *The Keepers*, a seven-part series that heavily promoted the theory of repressed memories by resurrecting and validating a previously dismissed Baltimore case from the early 1990s. The series purveys all the old stereotypes, including a psychologist who explains confidently: "Some things we experience are so unbearable and so painful that we shut them out." This popular series could undo years of good memory science in the public arena.

I have called this book *Memory Warp* principally because repressed memory therapy really does warp the brain, re-enforcing a synaptic network of false memories that can come to seem as true events that really occurred. "Warp" is a strong term for an amazing process. Who would believe that it was even possible to persuade otherwise normal people that they were raped for years in their childhood and completely forgot it? And that they would "remember" such prolonged abuse at the hands of their parents or trusted caregivers?

Warp can also refer to the lengthwise threads on a loom, around which other threads (the weft or the woof) weave to create a fabric. I explore the cultural context that spawned this late 20th-century witch hunt and that continues to foster it and other forms of sex panic. This was not an isolated phenomenon, but part of a cultural, ongoing *zeitgeist* that anthropologist Roger Lancaster identified in his 2011 book, *Sex Panic, and the Punitive State*, where he explored not only the repressed memory and Satanic ritual abuse craze, but paranoia over child kidnapping, the ill-advised war on drugs, mass incarceration, children "playing doctor" prosecuted as sex offenders and many other issues. "The never-ending parade of sex panics provides an important model – part metaphor and part blueprint – for the pervasive politics of fear," wrote Lancaster.

Although the overt practice of recovered memory therapy lessened, the mindset behind it never disappeared. The majority of therapists still believe in this pseudoscience; they are just hesitant to espouse it openly. And the general public has accepted the myth. A 2014 survey by psychology professor Lawrence Patihis and colleagues found that 81% of college students agreed that "traumatic memories are often repressed," and 86% thought that if someone had emotional problems and needed therapy, that they might well have suffered from childhood sexual abuse, even if they have no memory of the abuse; 83.9% of the general public thought that traumatic memories are often repressed. The majority of practicing psychotherapists thought so, too – 60.3% of clinical psychologists, 69.1% of psychoanalysts, and, for "alternative" therapists who practiced hypnotherapy or believed in internal personalities, the consensus on repressed memory validity went up to 84%. "The disconnect between psychological science and clinical practice is an unconscionable embarrassment (to the profession)," Walter Mischel, then president of the Association for Psychological Science, observed in 2009, and this disturbing data offers proof that he was correct.

So, the theory of repressed memory did not go away. It just went underground. Most therapists who specialize in trauma continue to believe in the theory of repression, and many continue to encourage clients to recall mythical abuse memories in order to get better. But, in general, they don't write about or brag about it and lawyers who call witnesses who have recalled such "memories" in court do not advertise their origins. While repressed memory excavation practices were banned from credible medical schools and hospitals, the practice continues in the offices of independent counsellors, social workers and even massage therapists.

In the process of writing this book, I contacted Professor Patihis at the University of Mississippi and asked if he might conduct a survey to show how many people had come to believe they had repressed memories of abuse. He agreed, and together we worked on the first-ever such survey, conducted through Amazon Mechanical Turk, an on-line method. Over 2,000 people completed the questions, and we will publish a detailed report in a professional journal in the near future. But I can report that the preliminary data are astonishing and alarming. We found that over 5 percent of those surveyed (ranging from 20 to 98) had recovered abuse memories in therapy. Adjusting the data for gender, ethnicity, and race reduces that to 4 percent. If that is representative of the adult U.S. population, that means that over 9 million people in this country have come to believe that they suffered childhood abuse but completely forgot it until they sought psychotherapy.

What shocked me about the survey results was the indication that the repressed memory epidemic still continues in an underground but robust manner. As expected, it seems to have peaked in the early 1990s, when 18 percent of those entering therapy retrieved abuse memories, and declined in a tsunami of lawsuits and licensing revocations from 1994-1997. But in the current decade, starting in 2010, eight percent of those seeking therapy came to believe they were abused as children, without previous memories.

Many of the anonymous comments were equally disturbing. A 26-year-old woman who took the survey wrote, for instance: "I believe I have repressed memories from trauma! I am highly suspicious of something that may have happened, but I am not sure and have no memory. If this young woman seeks out a "trauma therapist," she is likely to find her sought-after abuse memories.

In 2014, investigative journalist Ed Cara wrote about the Castlewood Treatment Centre in Missouri, which specialized in eating disorders but ended up convincing a number of patients, well into the 21st century that they harboured repressed memories and multiple personalities and that they had been in

Satanic cults. "The belief that hidden memories can be 'recovered' in therapy should have been exercised years ago," Cara wrote. "But the mental health establishment does not always learn from its mistakes – and families are still paying the price."

A woman in a Ph.D. programme in clinical psychology at a well-known university wrote to me long after the repressed memory epidemic had subsided. She preferred to remain anonymous, so I will call her Barbara. "I have been shaken by the lack of awareness of this problem (recovered memory therapy/false memories) at the centres where I have been trained. Most therapists I know claim to maintain neutrality regarding memories, but they also believe that massive repression exists in some or many cases. In addition, there are still so many young women and men who continue to come to therapy looking for reasons for their pain, and my experience is that some will go the way of abuse memories, even if the therapist does not. In my short time as a student therapist at this university's health centre, I was asked by clients more times than I would have ever expected if forgotten abuse might be a cause of their unhappiness. I still see copies of *The Courage to Heal* on my colleagues' bookcases."

Barbara didn't learn much about this issue in grad school. "Honestly, I don't remember much instruction about recovered memories at all, except for a brief mention during a psychopathology class that the diagnosis of DID (dissociative identity disorder, the new name for multiple personality disorder) is controversial." A belief in multiple personalities, allegedly created to forget horrendous memories, represented a kind of lunatic fringe during the repressed memory epidemic – yet it remains enshrined in the *Diagnostic and Statistical Manual of Mental Disorders*, the psychiatric bible.

One of the social workers with whom Barbara worked still believed in recovered memories and "stressed to me that she feels it's important to remain open to what the client brings." At another walk-in clinic, there was a social work student who "spoke openly about the memories her clients were uncovering and spoke proudly about having helped a client to realize that what she'd interpreted as a physical problem was actually a body memory." Indeed, in 2014 Bessel van der Kolk, the chief proponent of the idea of a "body memory," published the book, *The Body Keeps the Score*, which continued to promote the dangerous idea that "the body remembers what the mind forgets." The book received rave reviews, even in journals such as *Nature* and *New Scientist*, despite the fact that it contains two chapters espousing a pseudoscientific belief in massive repression/dissociation.

Linda Ross, whom I called "Robin Newsome" in the second edition of *Victims of Memory,* is one of the few therapists who once believed in repressed memories and has had the courage to go public to try and undo the harm, on National Public Radio's *This American Life* programme. She told me about the first time she met parents who had lost all contact with their children because of alleged repressed memories:

In the fall of 1993, I attended my first local FMSF meeting. I wasn't sure what to expect. These were the accused, after all. I remembered all that I had learned about how all perpetrators are in denial. I expected a room full of defensive parents. What I found instead was a group of sad and shocked parents who asked the same question their daughters asked: "How could she do this to me?" I had been so supportive of women with repressed memories, but I had never once considered what that experience was like for the parents. Now I heard how absolutely ludicrous it sounded. One elderly couple introduced themselves, and the wife told me that their daughter had accused her husband of murdering three people. Another woman had been accused of being in a Satanic cult that had used babies for sacrifices. This woman in a pink polyester suit was supposed to be a high priestess. The pain in these parents' faces was so obvious. And the unique thread was that their daughters had gone to therapy. I didn't feel very proud of myself or my profession that day.

Once Ross realized what harm she had done, she went back to her former clients to try and undo the damage. She believes that most therapists and ministers are still afraid to cast doubt on recovered memories. "If someone came to their pastor saying that they had thought they has been a horse thief in a former life," she says, "the pastor would say, 'As Christians, we don't believe in reincarnation.' And the same thing would happen if they remembered being abducted by aliens. But if they said they went to a therapist and had begun to recover abuse memories, the pastor will say, 'really? Can we pray for you?' They would completely believe it."

There is a high-profile case that provides alarming (and surprising) evidence that repressed memory is alive and well and continuing to do damage in our legal system. It turns out that many of the allegations against Jerry Sandusky, the ex-Penn State football defensive coach, were based on repressed memories. "The doorway that I had closed has since been reopening more," an alleged victim testified at the trial in 2012. "Through counselling and different things, I can remember a lot more detail that I had pushed aside than I did at that point." When I contacted him after the trial, he told me: "Actually both of my therapists have suggested that I have repressed memories. My therapist has suggested that I may still have more repressed memories that have yet to be revealed, and this could be a big cause of the depression that I still carry today."

There is compelling evidence that repressed memories were responsible for many of the Sandusky allegations, including Aaron Fisher, Victim Number One. It is a complex case which involves not only repressed memories but a media blitz, police and civil lawyers scouting for alleged victims, and millions of dollars awarded to troubled young men. It requires its own book, which I have recently finished – *The Most Hated Man in America: Jerry Sandusky and the Rush to Judgement* (Sudbury Press, 2017).

With *this* book, I am sounding an alarm and re-educating professionals and the general public about how memory actually works. *Memory Warp* provides a much-needed history lesson about how, in the late twentieth century, several million families – my educated estimate, though no one can establish firm statistics – were destroyed by an epidemic of false memories of sexual abuse.

Some accusing adult children retracted their repressed memory allegations, while others established uneasy contact but never apologized. In all too many cases, however, elderly parents have died without ever seeing their children again. "I am now 93 years old and having a very hard time," wrote one man in 2015. "The reason is that my wonderful wife passed away recently. Her last words were 'Where are my daughters?' Then she looked at me and said, 'I love you.' Then she closed her eyes. She was 85 years old. We have not seen or heard from our daughters for 23 years."

For years, the False Memory Syndrome Foundation, founded by Pamela and Peter Freyd in 1992, provided a well-researched newsletter and support system for families shattered by repressed memory allegations. The FMSF Newsletter offered updates and information on the latest scientific papers on memory and suggestibility, and back issues remain available online. But the Foundation is winding down, shifting primarily to a Facebook page, the False Memory Syndrome Action Network. In November 2016 Freyd wrote that she expected her organization to continue for only a few more years. "We continue to receive a small but steady stream of calls for help from families and questioning patients, and occasional calls from the media, students or attorneys." But the massive attention to the repressed memory disaster of the late 1980s and early 1990s has clearly passed. Still, Freyd continued, "We wish we could say that the constellation of beliefs that were the foundation of the recovered-memory phenomenon had disappeared, but the reality is that those beliefs linger in some segments of the population."

Freyd's wording implied that only a small minority still believe in repressed memories. But, as I've pointed out here, it is not just a fringe group that continues to support this discredited theory. It is the majority of the population. In other words, critical thinkers and multi-million-dollar lawsuits may have won the scientific and legal battle over false memories, but they appear to be losing the long-term "memory wars," as Frederick Crews called them. This book is a much-needed corrective.

THE BRITISH FALSE MEMORY SOCIETY

Introduction

In the previous chapter, Mark Pendergrast described how the repressed memory epidemic began in the United States during the late 1980s and early 1990s. The following chapters considers how the epidemic spread across the water from the US to the UK. I have utilised source material formerly housed in the archive of the British False Memory Society, including several thousand case files and contemporaneous newsletters published by the BFMS over a 30-year period from 1993 to 2023 when the society closed because of a lack of funding. These chapters also draw on earlier BFMS book publications – *Fractured Families: the untold anguish of the falsely accused* (BFMS, 2007) and its sister publication *Miscarriages of Memory: Historic abuse cases – a dilemma for the legal system* (BFMS, 2010). Additionally, the BFMS website contained a vast historiography about the repressed memory epidemic which provided useful background context for this project. Together, these sources illuminate popular perceptions about memory and belief in repressed memories which continue to endure today.

In the criminal justice system in the UK, complainants are granted – controversially – lifetime anonymity. It is a criminal offence to identify complainants, who are commonly referred to as 'victims.' Therefore, names have been changed. I have taken an editorial decision to not use ellipses in quotations. This is a book about the repressed memory epidemic (to coin Mark Pendergrast's term) and its devastating consequences for several thousand UK families. Chapter 11, the first study of its kind, analyses 30 years of data from the BFMS archive and attempts to quantify the legal impact of false memory-type allegations. It analyses trends and patterns over three decades including the number of cases taken on by the BFMS, and the number of these cases which entered the criminal justice system, interrogating prosecution, and conviction rates. In total, 227 BFMS members were convicted at trial; these dry statistics ought to cause alarm. The criminal justice system has failed these families, and the catastrophic impact of these wrongful convictions is life changing.

The case studies set out in this book shed light on the psychological makeup of accusers. In every single case I have been involved with since coming into post in 2014, the poor mental health of the accuser has featured prominently. Yet, this is rarely acknowledged by the criminal justice system. Nor are false memories. When it is recognised, the standard approach from counsel for the prosecution is to put the cart before the horse proclaiming that psychological illness is a by-product of childhood sexual abuse. As Dr Peter Naish has written, "Some therapists are convinced that all manner of dysfunction in adults are clear indicators that they were abused. This reasoning is as foolish as the following: 'People with malaria have a fever. Mary has a fever, so Mary must have malaria.' This is a logical fallacy which has destroyed families all over the world."

The criminal courts in the UK remain sceptical about memory expert witness testimony. This view was endorsed by the Criminal Court of Appeal (CCOA) in R v Bowman. "Essentially the professor's evidence of the results of research into memories goes little further than is common sense and well within the normal human experience."

In this pivotal 2006 ruling, (R v Bowman – EWCA Crim 417, 2 March 2006, paragraph 168), the CCOA ruled that memory expert witness testimony was inadmissible. This was an appeal by Thomas Bowman against a conviction for murdering his wife in 1978. The trial was based on recovered memories involving Bowman's daughter who entered therapy, aged 26, two decades after his wife passed.

Speaking on *BBC Radio 4s Law in Action* in 2008, retired judge, Gerald Butler, provided a damning assessment on memory expert witnesses:

I think, frankly, that it is a ridiculous suggestion (regarding memory expert witness testimony). We do have experts who can be very helpful. There are handwriting experts, and of course there are DNA experts who have turned out to be of immense value in the courts. But we also have juries who are there in order to use their common sense and when it is a situation that you weigh up a witness's evidence and decide whether she or he is telling the truth or that she or he has a faithful recollection of what has taken place, this is essentially a matter for the jury. It is not a matter for an expert.

The Code for Prosecutors is instructive. Revised in May 2022, following a consultation exercise (the BFMS were not consulted). In a section on Pre-Trial Therapy, it states that,

There is no substantive evidence that therapy will generate false memories. Further, some victims do in fact remember details of the abuse many years later; these are not false memories but rather real memories that had until that point been repressed.

This assertion is incorrect. However, it will make it even harder for an accused person to receive a fair hearing in future cases involving alleged repressed memory-type accusations.

Childhood Sexual Abuse

Before we explore the formation of the BFMS, it is pertinent to pause for a moment and to consider childhood sexual abuse (CSA) which is widespread, and common to all cultures. CSA may result in significant lifelong psychological harm. "A recent study by *UNICEF* and *Save the Children* estimates that one in five Filipino children are now at risk of sexual exploitation, putting the grim figure close to two million" (Laura Bicker, *BBC News Manila*, 29 November 2022). According to the NSPCC, in 2014 "over 3,000 children in the UK were identified as victims of sexual abuse, and one in 20 children in the UK have been sexually abused." One in three of those abused never disclose the abuse to anyone. There are many reasons for not disclosing abuse – not least that victim and perpetrator may live in the same household; a perpetrator may commit abuse while in a position of authority; a victim may be embarrassed or afraid to disclose. For all these reasons, delayed reporting of childhood sexual abuse is common.

The BFMS abhorred child abuse, which is morally reprehensible. It supported the full application of the criminal law against perpetrators. I posit that there is a crucial distinction between victims who have always remembered abuse and those who claim to have recovered memories following therapeutic or psychiatric input. There are two distinct datasets which encompass genuine abuse (most allegations) and recovered memories (a significant minority of cases). Some false allegations, of course, may be malicious occurring in contested child family court proceedings and/or in the context of an acrimonious divorce. Others may be motivated by the potential of monetary gain in civil lawsuits or through lodging an application to the Criminal Compensation Authority. There may be overlap in some cases with each of these elements. The focus of this book largely (but not exclusively) concerns wrongful allegations generated in psychological therapy.

Adult Children Accusing Parents (ACAP)

In 1992, an article in the American press drew a huge response, after a group of accused parents in the US attended a meeting with professionals from the University of Pennsylvania and John Hopkins University and the False Memory Syndrome Foundation (FMSF) was formed. The appointment of a scientific advisory board led to critical scrutiny of the social movement in which these therapeutic theories and practices were emerging. The rationale being offered by therapists and their designated forms of treatment began to be challenged.

In Britain, the turning point was 1990 when the British edition of *The Courage to Heal* appeared and, following the American experience, a belief arose that 'repressed memories' of sexual abuse were commonplace. After the first FMSF conference in Philadelphia in the spring of 1993, accused parents who attended from the UK met and formed an organisation which was to become the BFMS. The society initially began life as Adult Children Accusing Parents (henceforth ACAP). The remit of ACAP was pinpointed in the very first newsletter published in May 1993:

ACAP is a group of parents searching for an understanding of a new phenomenon. Our shared tragedy results from an adult son or daughter making a false claim of childhood sexual abuse. The group is promoting research into false memories and by publicising the existing knowledge of the problem, it is hoped that the rising tide of these false accusations can be stemmed. By placing our case histories and the growing body of academic literature in front of the public, we will try to alert psycho-therapeutic professionals, social workers, mental health workers and the legal profession to the dangerous practices now migrating across the Atlantic from America.

We must acknowledge that childhood sexual abuse does exist, and many caring agencies are helping the victims overcome the damage caused. ACAP does not wish to detract in any way from their efforts. We hope that our work will ease their burden as the different problems facing adult children and their families come to be recognised.

Our children are different because they claim that they had no knowledge of their abuse from the time it happened until the time they "recovered" their memories of it, decades later. This memory recovery was instigated by a therapist, a psychiatrist, a doctor, or a counsellor, who had been approached for help with an unrelated problem. Often, our children were encouraged by them to read "survivor" literature, including, in many cases, the American book, *The Courage to Heal*.

However, the problem for adults who were abused in a systematic way as children is that they can never forget their abuse. They often have a sense of shame and suffer guilt because they feel that it must have been their fault. Sympathetic therapy can help them come to terms with their feelings, but the trauma of their childhood will never be forgotten.

ACAP was founded by a retired British naval officer, Roger Scotford. He was an accused parent struggling to make sense of

the nightmare which had engulfed his family. In the summer of 1993, Roger wrote:

Here is our second newsletter, produced after a month which has seen our membership rise by over one hundred families. It has come as a considerable surprise that there are so many cases of claimed wrongful accusations coming to light after such relatively sparse publicity.

ACAP is preparing an application to the Charity Commission. It is our intention to promote and fund research into False Memory Syndrome (Editor – as it was then labelled).

We cannot say it firmly enough that we know that childhood sexual abuse does occur and everything possible should be done to minimise its occurrence. The victims should be helped to come to terms with the consequences and the perpetrators should be punished.

Formation of the British False Memory Society

Roger Scotford achieved enormous media success in raising awareness about alleged repressed memories. But, on another level, the opening of Pandora's box resulted in an increasing caseload which was proving difficult to manage. Staffing the helpline was challenging, and the caseload was increasing. Consequently, Madeline Greenhalgh (who would later take over Roger Scotford's role as director of the BFMS) was recruited by Scotford in 1993, to assist with this ever-increasing role. Madeline has described how she became involved with the BFMS and the unusual recruitment process:

"How did this work start and how did I come into this world of false memories? At the time, I was a working mother with two teenage children. I had a background of working for charities – one offering horticultural therapy for disabled people and one training volunteers for work in developing African countries. It was 1993 and I was contacted by an employment agency to consider the post of deputy director collaborating with Roger Scotford, the founder and director of the organisation called, Adult Children Accusing Parents. The title simply summed up what was happening. It had happened to him; he was an accused father looking for an academic understanding as to how and why this was happening. He found Professor John Money, who was a professor of paediatrics and medical psychology at John Hopkins University, Maryland, who introduced him to Dr Pam Freyd who had started the False Memory Syndrome Foundation in 1992 after she and her husband had been accused. She informed Roger about a large meeting of grey-haired Americans who were facing the same problems Roger had encountered. He attended returning to England to give a powerful interview to the *Daily Telegraph*. The response was amazing with lots of related stories being told. That was the beginning of our membership organisation. After an inaugural meeting of all those interested in meeting up, it was agreed to set up a registered charity and trustees were chosen.

Back to my interview – it was a shock! I walked into the room while Roger was taking a first call from a father who had been accused; the conversation was extraordinarily frank, and I proceeded cautiously. Cleverly, Roger recognised that I had never been confronted with the subject matter openly discussed in his office and after an hour's chat he advised that I take away a number of academic articles (all American, at that time) about the development of therapeutic practices inciting recovered memories of childhood abuse, and to take a couple of weeks to consider the problem, to see if I wanted to work in the field. Once I had worked my way through the articles, I felt committed to join this organisation determined to help challenge this new threat to family life.

By 1994 we were applying for charitable status and changed the name to the British False Memory Society. We won three years of pump-prime funding from the Department of Health, although I clearly recall the problems we encountered in claiming the final tranche following the change of Government in 1997. It was all part of the development of a powerful divide between the burgeoning therapeutic industry and the academic exposure of the Memory Wars."

The purpose of the BFMS

From the outset, the Society aimed to raise public awareness of the inherent dangers of false memory by disseminating relevant information through newsletters and articles; organising seminars and conferences; and assisting the media to produce suitable articles and programmes. During the period from 1993 to 1997 there were dozens of newspaper and magazine articles about false memory and the fractured families engulfed in this ticking timebomb.

In 1994 Richard Ofshe and Ethan Watters published *Making Monsters: False Memories, Psychotherapy, and Sexual Histeria* (1994). Esteemed members of the American scientific community reaped critical praise on this seminal publication, which won the Pulitzer Prize:

Dr Ofshe, who was based at Berkely University, California, gave a seminar in London on 10 October 1994 warning about the dangers of 'recovered' memories comparing it to the lobotomy era. Many BFMS members attended the seminar which was warmly received. One of whom wrote the following short note to the society:

From a mother

I felt I had to write to you to thank you for arranging the seminar in London last Monday. We found it so helpful, and it has given me renewed strength to cope personally having mingled with so many people with the same problems.

Although obviously I had realised that I was not alone, to hear of the professional concern expressed by the panel, and particularly by Dr Ofshe, gave me tremendous hope that perhaps one day many of us will be reunited with our children, and come what may, it enabled me to understand how this dreadful accusation came to be made. Because doubtless like so many, I have been tormented by the thought, 'what could I have done to bring this state of affairs about?' when in fact, as Dr Ofshe pointed out, our children simply knocked on the wrong door at the wrong time.

Once again, thank you so much for all you do at BFMS. I'm sure the seminar last week has made so many accused members feel so much stronger. My own daughter is now receiving treatment at her local hospital, and she has asked that we (both myself and my husband) only contact her in emergencies, for the four months which is due to end on December 7th – presumably that is the date her session of treatment ends. I am allowed to write to my little granddaughters 'occasionally,' but she did send me a birthday card and a lovely photo of the children, which gives me great hope. The last time I was able to speak on the phone to my granddaughters was on May 20th, the youngest's birthday, and she said, "It's long days since we came to your house, Nanny." I just hope one day I can show them the love I have for them.

In a similar vein, a wife of an accused husband wrote:

My husband died last January after suffering a massive stroke. He and I began to have high blood pressure at about the time of our daughter's accusations.

This stress had been going on for several years and we'd both been put on medication for that condition. He was depressed. He sighed and said, "Well, I guess there's nothing more I can do." Our daughter had returned his last letter to her unopened, writing on the envelope, 'Unacceptable mail; return to sender.'

There is no doubt in my mind that the stress he had suffered from her false accusations was at least partially responsible for his premature death. He was a vigorous healthy, 66-year-old man.

Now I am trying to cope with the loss of my dear, loving husband of 46 years while, at the same time, struggling to overcome the bitterness I feel toward my daughter and her therapist. The tragedy of this almost overwhelms. In my opinion, the therapists who are promoting these false memories are guilty of murder!

A Widow

Another member wrote:

Thankfully, we no longer need the literature you sent but we have passed it on to someone who does. Our daughter came to see us asking for our forgiveness. She said that even when she was making her accusations, she knew they were not so, but she had become so desperate to please her therapist that she said whatever she felt the therapist wanted to hear. It was exactly as your phone volunteer had told me. When our daughter went with totally unrelated problems, she was told they had to be caused by abuse even if she couldn't remember it. We will always be grateful for your help.

A Mum and Dad

In October 1994, The Australian Psychological Society issued the following (edited) guidelines to therapists and psychologists:

Guidelines relating to recovered memories.

These guidelines set forth conclusions and recommendations designed to safeguard psychologists and clients who are dealing with reports of recovered memories.

Scientific Issues

Memory is a constructive and reconstructive process. What is remembered about an event is shaped by what is observed of that event, by conditions prevailing during attempts to remember, and by events occurring between the observation and the attempted remembering. Memories can be altered, deleted, and created by events that occur during and after the time of encoding, and during the period of storage, and during any attempts at retrieval.

Memory is integral to many approaches to therapy. Repression and dissociation are processes central to some theories and approaches to therapy. According to these theories and approaches, memories of traumatic events may be blocked out unconsciously and this leads to a person having no memory of the events. However, memories of these traumatic events may become accessible at some later time. Although some clinical observations support the notion of repressed memories, empirical research on memories generally does not. Moreover, the scientific evidence does not allow general statements to be made about any relationship between trauma and memory.

"Memories" that are reported either spontaneously or following the use of special procedures in therapy may be accurate, inaccurate, fabricated, or a mixture of these. The level of belief in memory or the emotion associated with the memory does not necessarily relate directly to the accuracy of memory. The available scientific and clinical evidence does not allow accurate, inaccurate, and fabricated memories to be distinguished in the absence of independent corroboration.

Psychologists should recognise that reports of abuse long after the alleged events are difficult to prove or disprove in the majority of cases. Independent corroboration of the statements of those who make or deny such allegations is typically difficult, if not impossible. Accordingly, psychologists should exercise special care in dealing with their clients, their family members, and the wider community when allegations of past abuse are made.

Psychologists should be alert to the ways that they can shape the memories reported by clients through the expectations they convey, the comments they make, the questions they ask, and the responses they give to clients. Psychologists should be alert that clients are susceptible to subtle suggestions and reinforcements, whether those communications are intended or unintended. Therefore, psychologists should record intact memories at the beginning of therapy and be aware of any possible contagion effects (e.g., self-help groups, popular books). Psychologists should be alert to the role that they may play in creating or shaping false memories.

British Psychological Society (BPS) – Recovered Memory Working Party Report

The BPS announced findings of its Working Party at a televised press conference in London on 12th of January 1995. The BFMS responded:

We applaud the Working Party for attempting to lay down some guidelines for therapists to follow, and whilst we acknowledge that by its very nature, any report on memory will be fraught with uncertainty, the lack of evidence, research, corroboration, and scientific thinking in the body of the report is astounding. It uses the results of a survey of BPS therapists to substantiate the notion that recovered memories are accurate. It does so on the basis that they are highly trained individuals who therefore cannot be wrong.

However, just as we go to press, the survey results have been published in the May issue of the Psychologist. It turns out that 97% of the polled therapists believe that recovered memories of childhood sexual abuse are sometimes, usually, or always essentially accurate. But there is another staggering piece of information, not even hinted at by the working party report; 97% also believe that Satanic Ritual Abuse recovered memories are essentially accurate. What a shame their survey didn't pose the question; 'do you believe that recovered memories of the womb/from past lives/of alien abduction are essentially accurate?' Then we would have a fuller picture of the dubious beliefs of BPS therapists, only 25% of whom returned the survey.

In a 1995 BFMS Newsletter Professor Lawrence Weiskrantz expressed his views on the report.

Comments on the Report of the Working Party of the BPS on "Recovered Memories"

It was prudent of the BPS to set up a Working Party (WP) to report on the widely debated question of "Recovered Memories," and one can applaud its decision to do so. My comments concern its contents and conclusions. I am not personally involved in any aspect of accusations or abuse, but I have agreed (along with several other senior academics) to respond to an invitation to serve on an advisory committee for the British False Memory Society to suggest possibilities of conducting relevant research and for having rational discussions with the professionals and the public. Anyone having contact with any of the distressed families cannot fail but to have a concern about the issues.

The WP had a real and rare opportunity to make a contribution to a problem of deep clinical and social importance. Instead, I am afraid, it has messed up. After a conspicuous spell of silence, it has produced a report that will mollify its own constituents, i.e., BPS accredited therapists, but makes no significant practical contribution. Aside from issuing common-sense "guidelines" to therapists (for this, at least, we can be grateful), rather later than those of some other professional bodies in the world, it has done little to redress anxieties that have been widely expressed about particular clinical practices. I fear that some of its statements, quite unnecessarily, will polarize and add heat to the debate, which many of us have tried to avoid.

The survey is based on responses to a brief one-page questionnaire by 810 Chartered Psychologists, to obtain "preliminary answers." When will less "preliminary" answers be sought? Surprisingly, we are told the number of respondents, but not the number to whom the questionnaire was sent, so we do not know the proportion of respondents nor their representativeness, nor indeed anything at all about them (nor will the public know what is meant by BPS accreditation of therapists). The analysis of the Survey in their report occupies just 15 lines, which justifies the comment that it should be regarded as "preliminary." Even the reporting of the results of this simple "preliminary" report is itself incomplete. The serious flaw in the report is evident, however: instead of focusing on real points that give rise to anxiety in clinical practice, it attempts to give a global view, as it were, of the BPS practitioners. It is of the variety, "x per cent prefer our brand of cat food." One transparently inadequate conclusion, positively endorsed by the WP without comment, is that "recovered memories are seen sometimes as usually 'essentially' accurate by nine out ten of the group." How is this judgement made (and how many responded "sometimes" and how many "usually")? Were the memories trawled by the therapists themselves? In which case they might be expected to judge their efforts positively. Was the judgement based on an effort to seek corroborative evidence? If so, how often, and with what outcomes? The Working Party itself dismisses the matter of seeking corroborative evidence as a "forensic" matter. That is an astonishing position to take. In effect, it is saying that the question of validation is for the police and the lawyers and not for the scientist! This is not to say that it would necessarily be within the remit of the WP itself to seek corroborative evidence, but it surely must endorse the scientific relevance to external historical truth, to seek it and to analyse it when possible.

What one wants to know, however, are not the therapist's "collective" views, but the prevalence and force of danger points. One such danger point is whether there are a significant number of respondents who use hypnotic regression to uncover traumatic memories, about which many anxieties have been expressed. The question is included in the survey, but there is no hint of the answer. But even if, say, 90% do not use such methods, 10% who do would be worrying. No one claims that all therapists are following unwise practice, or that all clients are being unwisely influenced. The issue is whether there are some who are. From this report we get no clue whatever. But there is something else worrying about the results that are reported. "Over ninety percent have seen clients in the last year who report child sexual abuse." What can one make of that? No one denies the dire consequences of CSA, and the need to deal with it severely by law and humanely by therapy. But is it the case that the 90% of BPS therapists specialise in CSA? Is it the case that (perhaps) a majority of clients who approach any "accredited" BPS practitioner have suffered from CSA? Such highlighted percentages do little to allay suspicion that these respondents include some who are zealously rooting out reconstructed or "metaphorical" CSA rather than real CSA from a woodpile. "About half the respondents had clients who at some time reported experiencing recovering a memory of CSA." And "more than one in five have at least one client in the last year who recovered a memory of CSA."

The WP were invited by the British False Memory Society to examine its records (in confidence). No acknowledgement is given of its open and continued cooperation. The WP spent a few hours examining (the now incomplete – the number has risen to 550) records of 200 cases. Some of these contained correspondence between the accusers and their parents.

Such correspondence must obviously be "sketchy and unsystematic." The hope by the BFMS must have been that the WP would seek further ways of finding out more about particular clinical practices that are claimed by them to lead to patiently undesirable outcomes, rather than any expectation that anguished but nevertheless informative correspondence by itself could be a final basis for a scientific analysis. One might have even hoped that the BPS would offer to find independent ways, given its authority, of examining the backgrounds of the claims of the accused families of the Society. There is no evidence that the WP discussed the situation widely with accused parents, if with any at all. Instead, it gratuitously takes a pot shot at the American False Memory Foundation, under the deeply misleading heading of "characteristics of verified abuse in adulthood." I understand that the FMF's records in the USA are open to examination on request, had the WP wished to do so. Instead of attempting any independent analysis, all the Report says is that "further documentation is needed by False Memory Societies in order to obtain a more reliable picture." It has been left to a charity, not the BPS, to support a project (by a senior member of staff of the Institute of Psychiatry and with approval of its Ethics Committee) to obtain further detailed documentation of the parents, and to glean information about therapeutic regimes and to draw whatever conclusions might be feasible about the accusers (Editor – Professor Gisi Gudjonsson's surveys of BFMS members are discussed in chapter 11). Until such proper demographic data are available it is premature to draw conclusions about the British data.

The full version of this article also appeared in the Therapist Magazine, the journal of The European Studies Institute. Winter 1994 Vol. 2. No 4.

Into the Brave New World – Madeline Greenhalgh

In 1999, Roger Scotford resigned as director of the BFMS. During the previous five years Roger had campaigned tirelessly to raise awareness about the false memory epidemic. Setting up the BFMS constituted an enormous task, which placed a heavy burden on his shoulders. "I'm tired, Madeline, do you want to take over? Think about it." With some trepidation, Madeline agreed. In her first editorial for a 1999 newsletter, she wrote:

Dear Friends,

The first months of my new position as director have flown by. It is an impossible task to follow in Roger Scotford's footsteps following his retirement. So much has been achieved in the first five years with Roger at the helm, so we are delighted that he has agreed to act as a Consultant to the Society. I hope though, that we can work together to take the Society into the future with the aim to ensure that never again will parents have to endure the devastation that false memories have brought upon their families. With unscientific beliefs still much in evidence among mental health professionals we do still have a long struggle on our hands! Only last week, a full-page article was published in the *Daily Mail* about a young woman who was diagnosed through a helpline counsellor as having Multiple Personality Disorder MPD (now known as Dissociative Identity Disorder). In the United States this diagnosis has caused very serious concerns; we do not want to see an epidemic of cases on our doorstep.

The process of retraction has also been of interest to a PhD Researcher in Portsmouth. James Ost (editor – deceased 2019) has carried out some research into retractor's experience of recovering and retracting abuse memories. He has found that the process of retraction takes substantially longer than the original recovery of "false memories" and with the presence of far less social pressure.

Some retractors who are now struggling to rebuild their lives since realising what has happened to them, have decided to seek redress through the legal system. The procedure is long and arduous, often starting with a formal complaint to the therapist's or clinician's professional body, possibly to the General Medical Council or the Health Ombudsman and ultimately, if there is no satisfaction, to the courts.

I have been overwhelmed by the cards and messages of support and encouragement that I have received. I have always valued contact with members and hope that you will continue to keep us up to date with any developments in your family and to contact us with your ideas and questions.

Speaking at the BFMS annual conference, a few years later, Greenhalgh delivered a speech which pinpointed ongoing concern about recovered memories:

Towards the end of the year, I was contacted by a 21-year-old woman, who believed she had recovered memories of severe childhood sexual abuse at the hands of her mother and father. She explained how she first began to doubt her memories after she had a flashback of her miscarriage – as the scenes flashed before her, she knew they were not a true reflection of the real event she had suffered the year before. This set her thinking that if these flashbacks of her miscarriage were false then all the rest of her sexual abuse flashbacks could be made up too. This young woman was marking the beginning of sorting out her life; she still has a long way to go before she fully understands why she made such vicious and devastating claims about her mother and father. During the past eighteen months she has become dependent upon daily calls to a 'survivors' helpline. She was advised to ring the helpline by her Community Psychiatric Nurse and with the survivor group's 'help' she has gone from believing she was abused as a child to taking on the notion that she was also involved in ritual abuse, that she murdered babies and that she is now the bearer of 63 alter-personalities. This helpline is open every day, except Sunday, between 6.00 and 8 00p.m. If she struggles with her dependency to ring them, managing to avoid the obsession to go over her narratives for the umpteenth time to see where they might lead her this time; the helpline staff will take the 'trouble' to ring her to ensure that she hasn't been 'got at' by the ritual abusers again.

These passages encapsulated the challenges facing the society following the first decade of its existence. As we moved into the 21st century, there was an expectation that science would triumph over pseudoscience. In hindsight, although commendable, this optimism was misplaced. The repressed memory epidemic, though weakened by the memory wars of the 1980s and 1990s, continued unabated. Bad therapy continued. Rationale analysis was suspended. Fringe therapy, especially, became an industry. This industry was oblivious to scientific enquiry and remains so to this day.

TWO CASE STUDIES

PRISCILLA

This case study was originally published in Victims of Memory by Mark Pendergast (Harper Collins, 1996), and later reproduced in Fractured Families (BFMS, 2007).

A homeopath and The Courage to Heal help Priscilla to believe that her physical ailments stemmed from repressed memories of sexual abuse. She calls her father to tell him that she needs to see him because of what she has 'remembered.' Puzzled and apprehensive, he drives for several hours to meet her.

On Thursday afternoon I arrived at Priscilla's London flat, and the door was opened by a young woman whom I didn't know who introduced herself as Lena. She said that she was there to help Priscilla and she ushered me into the front room of the flat. In the bay window there was a raised dais, and my daughter was sitting there, in a lotus position like a little Buddha. In the centre of the room was a large chair, and she motioned me to sit in the chair. Lena came in behind me, shut the door, and sat by it, like a guard.

Priscilla then said something like: 'I want you to listen to what I am going to say and what I'm going to read to you, and when I'm finished, I shall get up, leave this room, go into the garden, and you are to leave the house. I don't want you to say anything. I don't want you to ask any questions. I just want you to listen to me.'

She then started reading from a handwritten statement. The opening was a sort of preamble describing how she'd had a poisoned life until now, that she'd managed to strip away the poisoned outer layers of her personality, and she'd been able to discover her true inner self. She then explained the reasons she had those poisoned layers and preceded to tell me about the 'sexual abuse' that she had been subjected to when she was nine months old, two years, four years, eight years old. It was a complete shock to me.

I went numb. I could not believe what I was hearing. I remember thinking: 'This is not real; this couldn't be happening.' Pricilla moved into a second part to talk about the compensation she wanted to help her overcome the pain and suffering the supposed abuse had caused her. She needed psychotherapy for two more years. She needed a safe place to live. And at the end of each item, she gave a monetary figure. "So, the total is £70, 000,' but quickly added, 'I'll settle for £50, 000." I hasten to add I never paid her any money, other than to help pay for psychotherapy that I thought would help her.

Then Priscilla read out a letter from Davina Anivad, her homeopath. I subsequently got a copy of it, so I will read part of it to you. It is addressed, *To Whom It May Concern*. 'As a professional practitioner, I wish to state that all Priscilla Brightwell's symptoms, whether physical, mental, or psychological, are consistent with her being a survivor of father/daughter rape, over a continued period of time. I have a great deal of experience in working with people who have been abused as children, and sadly Priscilla is one of them. The healing only starts to begin with the re-surfacing of the memories.' Finally, Priscilla read the end of the letter: 'The abusive father, who could face many long years in prison, should seek help for himself and not deny the damage he has done to his daughter, whose safety was in his hands. He must not expect forgiveness from her.'

This whole scene lasted about half an hour. It seemed like an eternity, though. The only thing I said was at the end: 'Those things didn't happen, Priss.'

I left Prisilla's flat in a state of shock. I got into my van and drove round the corner to a phone box and rang up Rachel, my youngest daughter, who lived nearby. (My oldest daughter, Mary, was married and living abroad, so she wasn't part of this). I said: 'Rachel, I just had the most disastrous meeting with Priscilla,' and she said: 'Yes, I know. And I believe her.' So that was sort of a double blow. I haven't seen Rachel or Priscilla since.

When I got home, I contacted my ex-wife, Hannah, and arranged to meet her. Of course, she knew all about it. These accusations had been coming out for weeks, apparently. Hannah and I agreed we would seek proper therapeutic help for her. So, we found a well-recommended therapist in London, Stephanie Brent, at the London Institute.

However, I soon became very concerned that this woman had not made a proper diagnosis of their problems. She was treating them for the wrong disease. She was treating them as if they were victims of real childhood sexual abuse. There was some acrimonious correspondence between us which got nowhere. I was so outraged that she should call my daughters my 'ex-family.' In the end, I stopped paying for them to have therapy.

A year later, an acquaintance in America sent me a copy of an early False Memory Syndrome Foundation Newsletter. It was a revelation. It was the first ray of sunshine through dark clouds. I could clearly see that my daughters had been clobbered by this new seemingly American phenomenon called False Memory Syndrome. Naively and probably stupidly, I thought I only had to show Priscilla and Rachel the evidence of FMS and they would quickly see that they had become victims of it. I had not considered that I was not dealing with rational people. I sent them a copy of the newsletter and Melody Gavigan's early Retractor Newsletter. Then all hell broke loose.

Priscilla called and left a message on my answering machine. Her words rumbled out on to the tape in a bitter torrent. To me, the most important thing that came across from the tape is that she really believes that those things happened to her and has integrated it into her personality. If you met her, you wouldn't think that anything was wrong. She would seem perfectly normal. It's really frightening.

After a while, Priscilla wrote: 'Now Rachel has remembered too, but it's different.' I never discovered what the difference was exactly. So, I now have two daughters out there, seemingly believing that I did those terrible things to them, when of course I didn't. The whole thing is so stupid and implausible. There doesn't seem to be much I can do about anything. I honestly don't know how to help them realise that their nightmare images never actually happened.

PHOEBE

This case was first published in Miscarriage of Memory: Historic abuse cases – a dilemma for the legal system (William Burgoyne and Norman Brand eds. BFMS 2010), following the writer's talk to the 2008 BFMS annual general meeting. Phoebe describes her teenage experiences in a Child and Adolescent Mental Health Unit which led her to make false accusations of sexual abuse.

Childhood

I am the oldest of three children. I had a very happy, unremarkable childhood. I was unusually tall as a child and a specialist predicted I would be 6ft 3in by adulthood. My parents felt I would not be able to cope with the social complexities of being a very tall woman, and I had hormone treatment at the age of nine which induced early puberty with the goal of limiting my final height. At 11, I went to boarding school. I had experienced the hormone treatment itself as quite invasive, and its effects left me ill-equipped to deal with boarding school's tough communal living.

In retrospect, I would say that by the age of 12, I was clearly clinically depressed. Throughout adolescence and adulthood, I have suffered from recurrent depressive episodes which have not been precipitated by any particular external events. During these episodes I suffer significant insomnia, loss of appetite and nausea, flatness and despair. My poor eating was picked up by the school and I saw an eating disorder specialist. The sessions did not help me, and she referred me to a child and adolescent psychiatrist in the area of my boarding school. In her referral letter, she said:

P reveals very little to me and is obviously very loyal and wary of change. P is extremely conscientious, sensitive to other people's feelings and wanting to please.

Initial outpatient sessions with the psychiatrist

The sessions with the new psychiatrist did not go much better. Though his early letters and notes are littered with references to depression, I do not remember anyone ever telling me this diagnosis, or what it meant. Nobody said to me: you are not the first person in the world to feel like this. The way you are feeling now is a recognised condition. When people feel like this they sit tight and wait it out. Because I did not know what depression was, or that I had it, I was frightened and desperate. I was also vulnerable to the suggestion that the onus was on me to explain why I was feeling like this. I had experienced some significant life events. A close family friend had died. There was the hormone treatment and its effects. I had difficulties in my relationship with my sister. I was experiencing the usual teenage struggles with my parents. I was acutely aware, however, that they did not account for how I was feeling. Neither did they appear to be sufficient explanations for the psychiatrist, who wrote to my doctor:

There are probably other factors of relevance in P's history, but at this stage it is hard to be clear what they are.

Because the psychiatrist's notes do not include his side of the conversation regarding how he responded to the problems I did reveal, or how he approached determining these 'other factors,' I can only say *how I felt*. I felt that he believed that my difficulties were caused by some significant life event, which he believed I was concealing. I felt under pressure to account for the depth of my unhappiness, and that the real problems I did offer up were not considered sufficient. I remember lying awake the nights before the sessions, wondering what I would be able to offer the next day. Beyond this, I also began to believe myself that there must be One Big Reason why I was feeling so awful, and my failure to find one only added to my panic and despair.

Beyond mentioning these everyday problems, which I did spontaneously and without a high degree of specific questioning, I was largely silent. To be fair, I was giving indications in those early days that there were things I could not talk about. I was desperately struggling – and utterly failing – to deal with the fact that I was gay. It was causing me great distress, but I did not feel able to talk to the psychiatrist or anyone else about it. At the General Medical Council (a GMC hearing brought by P's parent against her psychiatrist), these indications that I had something more to talk about were used as justification for the psychiatrist's belief that something else significant had happened to me.

The psychiatrist decided I would benefit from antidepressants. I believe we discussed that the tablets were dangerous in overdose, though I can find no record of this discussion. I had direct access to the tablets and, feeling increasingly desperate, I took too many. I was admitted to the paediatric ward of the nearest hospital and then to the psychiatrist's Adolescent Unit on the same site.

First impressions of Unit

It is difficult to describe the shock of the exposure to the world of the Unit. It was like nothing I could ever have imagined. All the rules of the normal world were suddenly turned on their head. Everyone was intent on injuring or killing themselves, while staff tried half-heartedly to stop them. I saw a patient with terrible scarring to her arms on my first day there, and my first thought was to wonder who had done that to her, when it dawned on me that she had done it to herself. I began self-harming very quickly – it made perfect sense in that environment - which was so restricted that all the normal healthy coping strategies were unavailable. I was able to secretly obtain razor blades from other patients who had brought them onto the unit. It was a strange environment in which problems became infectious and everyone's misery fed off everyone else. At lunch that first day, having always been a fussy eater, I couldn't eat the food. I remember a particularly aggressive member of staff accusing me of having an eating disorder. I couldn't reply. I was blinking back the tears thinking "no, I just don't eat this; ask my mum, she'll tell you". And I was hit with the realisation that my mother wasn't there, and that not even she could help me now.

I was by far the youngest patient, and I was out of my depth. I understand that 'trauma' is a loaded word, but I do not think it is an overstatement to say that I was traumatised by my sudden submersion into inpatient psychiatric care, at a time when I was at my lowest and most vulnerable and had no resources to draw on. A different psychiatrist reported seeing me smile for the first time six weeks after my admission.

Again, because there are no records of the general attitude on the Unit, I can only talk about how I personally perceived it. I felt there was a strong message which said: you can't leave here until you're better. We can't help you get better unless we know what's wrong. You must give us a reason for why you're feeling like this. A nursing note from early in my admission recorded:

Very tearful. No explanations. Answering direct questioning.

That is how it started. I had no explanations to offer.

First allegations and response

I was deteriorating. In the days leading up to the allegations I was seeing the psychiatrist at least once a day. I had been in the Unit a few weeks by then. There were two sessions the day the first allegations emerged. When I looked at my medical records, I was surprised by how easy it is to see how the allegations arose, and I share that now.

P very withdrawn – not talking. I talked about her discussion that it felt that there were people who had let her down, people who had made promises to her who had somehow or other then gone away. Reminded P she said there were more people. I asked P how many other people. She said one. I asked whether adult or child and after a lot of hesitation P said – adult. Male or female? Again, after a lot of hesitation P said male, in a whisper. Was it family? No, it wasn't. Was it someone P had known a long time? No, it wasn't. Was it somebody in the country? No, it wasn't. Was it somebody at her primary school? No. Was it someone at her secondary school? No. Was it someone in London? Silence. I suggested to P that I guessed that it sounded as if it was somebody in London. Given that it was neither family nor school and it was clearly somebody else, I wondered if perhaps it was somebody medical. P agreed that it was. I asked whether 'it' had happened once or on several occasions? P said it did. I wondered where, given that it was a male doctor.

I'm aware that P has only seen one male doctor. P agreed this is the case. I asked P when she first saw the doctor. P said when she was eight. I then asked P when she first felt unconformable. P said when she was nine. P declined to talk further about what had happened. I suggested to P that I see her again shortly to talk about it further.

The psychiatrist clearly determined the agenda that day. Me 'being let down' became 'it' which became me 'feeling uncomfortable'. As far as I remember, I did not know what we were talking about. Where a question had two possible outcomes, I hesitantly selected one. When a question could be simply answered 'no', I did so. When we ran out of options, I said nothing. This was taken as a 'yes.'

I am at a loss to explain what happened that afternoon, because the entire afternoon session is described in five lines and a few words, and this is how they begin:

In this session P moved on to talk about how (followed by allegations of sexual abuse).

I do not know whether I made those allegations spontaneously or in the context of a question-and-answer session similar to that which had taken place earlier in the day. It was not pre-meditated. I have no idea what I was thinking. I had not planned to talk about the hormone treatment that day. I had not in fact known that the psychiatrist had known about it. The psychiatrist reported at the GMC that he had expected me to tell him how very uncomfortable I felt because of the appropriate [hormone treatment] examination. Yet in a summary of key events prepared by the nurse manager for the police, it was reported that in a session eight days previously the psychiatrist had "felt I was preparing to make a disclosure". At the GMC the psychiatrist was asked: "did you show your approval in any way to the extent that now perhaps you were getting somewhere with her, that you were able to move on with her, that sort of thing?". He replied, "I have little doubt that where (she) was able to speak, she got some sense of, well done, thank goodness you are talking". In the weeks following the allegation the clinical staff noted I would not be judged Gillick competent at this point.

Second allegations and context

One aspect of the Unit I found particularly extraordinary was the way in which patients were treated as if they were a serious risk to themselves during the week but were expected to go home and function normally at weekends. In the course of the weeks in the Unit I had contracted an interest in self-harm and suicide which left me feeling in serious danger of myself. It was a Friday, I was due to go home, and I was terrified that I wouldn't come back alive. I did not think this risk would be taken seriously (though later indications suggest that it may have been). I knew that I would be taken seriously if I said I was at risk from somebody else. I said my father had sexually abused me. These allegations, and all subsequent ones, were made to a member of the nursing staff who was giving me 'psychotherapy.' It wasn't calculation, it was desperation. I went to the children's ward for the weekend, as I would do every weekend for another year.

Final allegations

I went on to accuse two more men of abusing me. This happened in the context of a 'psychotherapy session.' The nurse asked a series of questions about the non-existent sexual abuse, things like how old I was when this first happened, and how many times had this happened, but then rather abruptly switched and asked if anyone else had done what my father had done. Again, I felt that what I had already said wasn't enough and that they expected more. I was exhausted and worn down, and in desperation, I named the only two other adult males in my life, knowing that this was my final offer, because there simply weren't any other candidates.

Ongoing confusion/retractions

That same month, and throughout the next, I made a series of retractions – verbally and in writing – to Unit staff, a social worker, and my guardian *ad litem*. I said repeatedly that I wanted to go home, and I set about trying to discharge myself. At the same time, I continued to give details of the alleged abuse and twice retracted my retraction. I also at times said the reason I wanted to go home was so I would be free to commit suicide.

I also made an early attempt to indicate that the Unit was making things worse, not better. One month after the initial allegations, the psychiatrist recorded:

P said she felt in some ways we weren't helping her to survive but more helping her get into a mess.

He also records his response:

I suggested that maybe the mess had been there at the outset and at least we knew now that she was in a mess.

By the next month, I had withdrawn from the staff at the Unit. I had realised there was no straightforward way out of this mess, and the only way forward was to die. The next evening, I left the Unit and attempted suicide. I didn't do it very well and I ended up back at the Unit. I was in it deeper than ever.

In the next couple of months, my relationship with the Unit changed dramatically. I stopped saying I wanted to go home and became very afraid to leave. I was utterly institutionalised and dependent on them. With the increasing distance and difficulties with my family, I came to see my keyworker and the nurse-psychotherapist, and my intense friendships with fellow inpatients, as my family.

My mental and physical state

My mental and physical state seriously deteriorated during my time in the Unit. I remained intermittently on sedative antidepressants. I was prescribed additional night sedation for long stretches, despite its highly addictive quality. The dosage was increased several times because I developed a tolerance to it. I was given an antipsychotic drug when I was acutely distressed. I also had regular medication. But despite the highly sedative effects of all this medication, I slept little or not at all. I sustained extensive scarring to my arms, legs, and torso over the year I was there. I was in constant pain from these wounds. My personal hygiene was very poor. I associated brushing my teeth with the 'abuse' I had suffered. I didn't wash or change my clothes because I was terrified of my own body. I stopped eating and drinking. By the psychiatrist's description, I was 'electively mute.' I felt suicidal for most of my time there. I truly believed that I would not leave the Unit alive. From the point of view of the Unit, my behaviour was difficult. I needed constant encouragement to take any fluids or food. I was not very compliant in taking my medication. I was able to abscond several times.

Continuing doubts and questions

Meanwhile, I continued to express my doubts about the abuse. Instead of retracting the allegations outright as in those first months, I began to ask questions. It was not that I was afraid of losing face, or that I felt that the legal and child protection processes had taken things out of my hands. I've already shown you that I was able to tell these people that the allegations were false. My dilemma was that I simply could not see *why* it would have arisen if it was not true, so I always fell back to the position that it must be true. I discussed this dilemma openly with the psychiatrist and Unit staff but did not get any satisfactory answers.

As time went on, the allegations became more and more part of my identity. I was identified by the staff and all the other patients as a victim of abuse. In my own head, fiction merged with reality and a fog of confusion descended.

The list of symptoms for survivors of abuse is so wide that of course I displayed several genuine 'symptoms.' I also developed others, became intensely afraid of men and feared my father coming to find me. I had bad dreams in which awful stuff did happen to me (probably because the whole thing was so on my mind). And as I repeatedly encoded and retrieved the things I had made up; they effectively *became* memories. Beyond that, the theory of sexual abuse had explanatory power – it made sense of things otherwise unexplained – and I fell for that.

External process and feelings about it

In the background of all this, there was a powerful external process involving child protection investigations and care proceedings, and it deeply affected me. My future was terribly uncertain and after two Emergency Protection Orders and a rejected application for an interim Care Order, stalemate was reached. A Care Order was finally granted 11 months after my admission to the Unit on the grounds that I was 'beyond parental control.' For the order to be granted, my parents had to concede that "the role played by each member of the family may have contributed to the reactive condition that P now exhibits."

About a month before I was discharged, the psychiatrist noted:

P was at the most depressed I have seen her for some time, crying and saying, "I want to go home, I just want to go home." P said that her year with us had been even more awful than the abuse before.

And from a week later:

Still saying she wants to go to London, wants to go home. When she tries to sleep main thought is "I want my Mummy." She desperately wants the abuse never to have happened.

Coming home

I was grief-stricken at the idea of losing my family permanently, and I began to think with my social worker about how I might gradually go home. This in turn threatened the foster placement, and it was terminated by the foster carer with little warning. When my social worker began talking about approaching new foster placements, I knew that I wanted to go home. I had only ever really wanted to go home. Now that I had nowhere and no one to hide behind, it was surprisingly easy to ask if they would have me. Their response was an unequivocal "yes, come home". All credit to my family. Two and a half years had passed since I had entered the Unit. I had had no contact at all with my father. I had regular strained contact with my mother and infrequent contact with my siblings. I had not been into the city where we lived. Yet the day the school holidays began, I walked into our family home, and we spent Christmas together. It really was that simple.

We had family therapy to talk in a controlled way about what had happened. My family were desperate for me to provide them with an explanation for what had happened. I couldn't because I didn't have one. I couldn't think about it or explain it even to myself. The family therapy gave them a way of letting me know what they had been through, which was desperately upsetting to hear. I did not reciprocate. If it was upsetting for me to learn how my parents had suffered, then how much more devastating would it be for a parent to learn of their child's suffering? Beyond my concern not to hurt my parents, I just had no words for what I'd experienced in the Unit.

After the family therapy ended, we basically got on with it! We didn't rake over the past at breakfast, lunch, and supper. In fact, we lived, largely, as if it had never happened. I am aware that cries of 'denial' will ensue from some quarters, but it wasn't like that. What I mean is that I re-entered my family on a totally equal footing. I was not held in debt, and I believe if I had been it would never have worked out.

I retracted the allegations to my family and to the social services, but I remained under a Care Order for another two years after I returned home. Three months before my eighteenth birthday, when the Care Order would have expired anyway, I applied to the court to have it lifted. It was a symbolic gesture.

Legalities since

I sued the psychiatrist, my key worker, the nurse who had administered the 'psychotherapy' and the nurse manager in 2004, a few weeks before the statute of limitations expired on my 21st birthday. The settlement negotiations centred around how much it might cost to have plastic surgery to repair the injuries I was able to inflict on myself during my time at the unit. In November 2004 the NHS Trust paid me £25,000 plus costs. They did not admit liability, but neither did they include a gagging clause.

My reason for speaking out

Sexual abuse is a very difficult subject. There continues to be a powerful voice which argues that allegations, especially from young people, are never false. As far as I can tell, the only way to establish that allegations can be untrue is if those who have made such allegations say so. So firstly, I want to say: I made allegations of sexual abuse which were utterly untrue. False allegations *do* happen.

Beyond that, I came here because I found out at the beginning of this year that things appear to remain largely unchanged at the adolescent unit in question. In 2004, five months before they settled my case, a sectioned patient was able to walk out of the unlocked door, with a noose around her neck from an earlier suicide attempt which staff had disrupted and hanged herself from a tree in front of the unit. Her inquest heard that she was "found with her arms in the branches as if she was trying to save herself." I am devastated but not surprised. I feel it was only a matter of time before a patient died in their care. If I had tried a bit harder, I would have died in their care.

I have since discovered the existence of a group of former and current patients of the Unit on a social networking site. I was appalled to see that young people who were only recently discharged are saying the very same things that my friends and I have said to each other about our time there in 1996. Although some of the comments are very positive about members of staff, they also say:

I was always anxious that if I wasn't self-harming/depressed or thin enough I would just be told to leave, even when at some level I wanted to stay because it felt like my only chance to 'get better.' It's not our illness' we have survived, it's (the Unit)!

Importantly, one of the expert witnesses called in the psychiatrist's defence at the GMC took issue with the idea that inpatient units are safe settings. He said, "One is constantly concerned about the highly risky behaviour of young people in adolescent units and certainly I do not regard it as a safe place." The other expert witness his defence called said: "It is very interesting how very often when young people come in, they get worse when they are on the inpatient unit. You could ask why."

I'd like to make it clear that I do not have a vendetta. I believe that what happened was bigger than one individual practitioner. I do think that the unit environment was a recipe for disaster. I think that what happened to me was one of the possible disastrous outcomes, but not the only one. Although it may be common knowledge among child and adolescent psychiatrists that adolescent units are not safe places, and that patients frequently deteriorate rather than improve, I do not think that it is widely understood by others. I know that my parents and I did not understand this prior to my admission. I wish we had.

Finally, I'm going to say a bit now about the things which went right. There was a happy ending because my family never let go. To me this was grace. There is a well-known Biblical story of a son who leaves home, squanders his inheritance, and returns only when he is destitute. Rather than resenting this, the father in the story sees his child when he is still far off and comes to welcome him home. That is how my family welcomed me.

I had a fantastic social worker who was prepared to swim against the tide and make herself unpopular on all sides by saying that it was time to stop arguing about what had and hadn't happened, what was imperative was to get me out of that Unit before it was too late.

I had a lovely, small, nurturing school which took a huge chance on me, accepting me directly from full inpatient-status and allowing me to skip the year I had missed while in the Unit.

I had a wonderful GP who was prepared to take sole medical responsibility for a patient with a formidable psychiatric history. I have not seen any kind of mental health professional since leaving the Unit, and I never will.

When I moved to London, I moved back in with my parents. My mother and I have breakfast together most mornings, and this time together has allowed us to make up for some of the time that we lost to the Unit and my years in Care. All our paths cross at home often, but we treasure the times when we are 'all together as a family.' We treasure them perhaps more than most families because we are so aware of how easily the ending could have been so different.

PART TWO

This chapter was originally published in Miscarriage of Memory: Historic abuse cases – a dilemma for the legal system (BFMS, 2010). Dr Mair (deceased 2022) was formerly a member of the BFMS Scientific and Professional Advisory Board. She was the author of Abused by Therapy, (Matador, 2013).

Creating nightmares: a short history of belief in ritual abuse

By Katharine Mair

What is ritual abuse?

The Ritual Abuse Information Network and Support Group (RAINS) has defined ritual abuse as 'sexual abuse occurring in the context of symbols or activities used repeatedly to frighten children.' Another definition is of abuse 'that occurs in ceremonial or circumscribed manner for the purpose of creating or manipulating already created alter mental states' (Noblitt and Noblitt, 2008). Neither of these definitions conveys the full horror of ritual abuse, which includes unspeakably disgusting, cruel, and criminal acts. These are said to be inflicted on children, often from infancy, by an organised group of people. Experiences supported by alleged survivors of this abuse include repeated rape, cannibalism, torture, being caged, being forced to participate in murders, animal mutilations and to ingest blood and other bodily fluids (Rutz et al., 2008).

How do we know about this? No traces of these crimes have ever been found, and none of the perpetrators have ever been brought to justice. We know of these crimes only through the testimony of alleged victims. Their testimony is nearly always produced after they have been in therapy, and this therapy will usually have followed a diagnosis of dissociative identity disorder (DID), a new name for what used to be called multiple personality disorder (MPD). People suffering from this disorder will spontaneously adopt different personalities, called alters, and speak as though they were completely different people. In therapy the client will talk, through via alters, to a therapist who understands this condition: This is long term psychotherapy; it takes years, probably a minimum of five years. It often takes two or more years to establish enough trust for the client to be able to disclose any important information (Miller, 2008).

Many people all over the world do believe they have suffered unimaginable horrors. Their therapists are convinced that powerful cults continue to terrorise both children and adults, and that only a few of their victims have the courage to seek help. For them this is an under-reported problem. Yet for others it is unbelievable that abuse on such a scale should be going on.

How did this come about?

Belief in ritual abuse can be traced to two very influential, best-selling books. Both tell the story of someone who discovered, while in therapy, that they had been abused from early childhood. The first was *Sybil* (Schreiber, 1973). This was written by a journalist and described the eleven-year long psychoanalysis of Sybil Dorset. Undertaken by Dr Cornelia Wilbur. During this therapy Sybil suddenly started assuming different personalities, switching between them in the apparently involuntary way that indicated multiple personality disorder (MPD). At this time MPD was still thought to be a very rare condition which had been linked in the past to possession by spirits or supernatural powers, and more recently to a variety pf psychological and neurological disorders. However, Dr Wilbur, who had welcomed the opportunity of undertaking the first psychoanalysis of a multiple personality, assumed from the start that Sybil's 'dissociation' resulted, not from any current problems she might have had, but from something in her past. She thought it must have started during childhood, possibly to distance Sybil from some trauma, and that to discover what this trauma was, she would have to ask the alternative personalities rather than the more reserved and rational host personality. These alters were encouraged to emerge, sometimes through hypnosis. Over time nineteen of them appeared – each was named and treated as a reliable informant. As expected, they spoke of childhood trauma, weird treatment by Sybil's mother, of which Sybil herself had been unaware.

The supposition that dissociation in an adult was a sign of severe childhood trauma established a model for treating MPD which has been followed to this day. Although full scale dissociation has always been seen in adults rather than children, therapists from now on believed that it started, long before it could be observed, in early childhood. From Dr Wilbur onwards any current explanations for dissociation were discounted, fostering instead the belief in childhood trauma, therapists encouraged the emergence of alters. Since these alters were often children, therapy would often involve an adult therapist talking to someone as if they were a child. The supposition was that alters had been adopted by abused children to protect them from full awareness of what was happening to them, and, most importantly, it was the alters rather than the host that held the memories of this trauma. From now on dissociation was no longer seen as an aberration to be controlled, but as a useful diagnostic indicator of childhood abuse.

Dr Wilbur never attempted to corroborate her conjectures and could get no peer reviewed psychiatric journal to publish her account of Sybil's treatment. However, her friend's second-hand, journalistic account became a best-selling book which was later made into a film. This was followed by a rapid increase in the diagnosis of MPD in the United States, and by 1980 it received official recognition by being included for the first time in the *Diagnostic and statistical manual of mental disorders* of the American Psychiatric Association (1980).

Sybil, even in her most dissociate state, never reported any ritual abuse. Was this because her therapist had never heard of it? No accounts of ritual abuse had appeared until 1980, when another best-selling book, *Michelle Remembers* (Smith and Padzer, 1980), gave us the first ritual abuse 'survivor' story, co-written with the psychiatrist who had uncovered the abuse. It detailed Michelle's sexual abuse and torture by a group of Satanists, including her parents. She had witnessed the ritual murders of babies and adults and had been made to eat the ashes of one of the victims; she had also been caged and tormented with spiders and snakes. Her torture had culminated in a visit from Satan, but she was saved by the intervention of the Virgin Mary and Jesus. Like Sybil, Michelle was found to have MPD. She revealed details of her abuse during therapy with Dr Padzer, who had previously worked in West Africa studying black magic rituals. These revelations were strenuously denied by Michelle's family, and no corroborating evidence was ever found. However, the book was a great success, achieving massive sales and publicity. Padzer then married Michelle, and together they profited from their new-found celebrity, appearing frequently on television and radio. Television talk shows in the US during the 80s started featuring topics such as "Satanic Breeders: Babies for sacrifice," and "Investigating multiple personalities: Did the Devil make them do it?" The Padzers frequently spoke at conferences, as experts on satanic cult ritual abuse (Victor, 1993).

In the US and Canada there was a growing interest both in ritual abuse and in MPD during the 1980s. Both were being reported with unprecedented frequency, and they increasingly went together. MPD had previously been dismissed by many psychiatrists and psychologists as iatrogenic, in other words, generated by therapists in suggestible, fantasy-prone clients (Merskey, 1992). However, by the end of the decade it was suggested that 1% of the population might have MPD (Ross, 1991). This was bad news, since by then many therapists believed that MPD was always a sign of severe child abuse. What made the news even worse was their belief that the truth about what had happened during childhood would be found, not by taking a careful history from their adult clients, nor by checking their background details, but by inviting the alters to tell them what they knew. Thus, clients would inform therapists while they were in an altered state of consciousness, often speaking with the voice of a child, sometimes after deliberately induced hypnosis. Therapists duly found their suspicions confirmed, so that gruesome tales of organised rape, torture, and murder, 'remembered' by their clients and recounted to their therapists, were leading to widespread anxiety about what might be happening to today's children. Preschool day centres were singled out for suspicion, and many very young children were intensively questioned or examined for 'signs of abuse.' Between 1984 and 1989 these investigations in the US led to the arrest of 100 men and women, of whom 50 were tried and convicted. All verdicts were later overturned, when the lack of any corroborating evidence was revealed (Victor, 1993).

Looking out for ritual abuse in the UK

Perhaps it was inevitable that what has been described as a 'moral panic' in North America should later spread to the UK and across the world. In 1989 Pamela Klein, a 'ritual abuse counsellor,' and Jerry Simandl, a youth officer with the Chicago police department, visited Britain and gave a series of presentations to professional working with adults and children. I attended one of these myself and experienced its powerful effect. Klein and Simandl spoke with authority, about the practice of Satanism, the organisation of the cults, and the methods used to intimidate their victims, confusing them so that their testimony would not be believed. At this meeting there was little time for reflection, or questions. It was not until much later that I wondered how they were able to be so specific about the practices of the Satanists since no cult members had ever been identified. Most of us had never heard of ritual abuse before, and probably most left in a state of shock, thinking as I did, 'Oh dear! I'll have to look out for this now.' In my work as a clinical psychologist, I did look out for it, and at one time I thought I had found it, until I realised that exposure to horror videos provided a far more likely explanation for this person's strange ideas.

Other professionals who had been at this presentation also looked out for ritual abuse and were more easily convinced. Included amongst them were child protection workers from

Rochdale, who were later responsible for removing 17 children from their parents. This action had been sparked off by bizarre stories of black magic and baby killing from a six-year-old boy. The children's responses to intensive questioning persuaded the social workers that they were all victims of an abusive satanic cult. A judicial inquiry later found that there was no evidence for this, the social workers and local police were severely criticised, and the children were eventually returned to their parents. Similar actions from social workers who had been alarmed by the testimony of ritual abuse 'experts,' led to children being removed from their parents in Orkney and in Nottingham. In each case no evidence of any ritual abuse was found, and the children were returned home (Waterhouse, 1990).

In 1991 the Government, concerned about all these happenings, commissioned Jean La Fontaine, an anthropologist, to carry out an investigation into the existence of ritual abuse cults in the UK. She found no evidence of the type of organised abuse that was being reported by various therapists, carers and alleged victims and considered that many of the 'disclosures' by young children were largely suggested by the adults interviewing them (La Fontaine, 1994).

Meanwhile, now that ritual abuse was in the public consciousness, professionals working with adults were also seeking and finding it. In the clinical psychology department where I worked, we had all by now heard of ritual abuse, but most of us saw no evidence of its effects in our clients. However, just a few of my colleagues did see such evidence, and they saw it repeatedly. Some of them were now quite upset at repeatedly having to listen to accounts of such gruesome abuse. When I raised this anomaly with a colleague, who at this time had several clients reporting ritual abuse, she explained that information about ritual abuse was 'often hesitatingly given, testing out the therapist with snippets of details.' Clearly it took a therapist who was able to join the dots. It also helped that they had no qualms about diagnosing MPD or, as it now came to be known, dissociative identity disorder (DID). Ritual abuse was only disclosed to the few psychologists in our department who did diagnose this condition. Before they started therapy, none of their clients had apparently been aware that they had been ritually abused as children.

RAINS conference 2001

After I retired, I remained curious about how some therapists were able to maintain their beliefs about ritual abuse. The La Fontaine report had now been published, as had studies by psychologists throwing doubt on the reliability of any 'memories' that were only recovered during therapy. There had been widespread concern about children wrongly taken into care, and parents who had been unjustly accused of horrible crimes. In 1993 the British False Memory Society had been established to support these parents, and to focus the concerns of many professionals working in this area.

It was therefore with interest that in 2001 I attended a conference organised jointly by RAINS (Ritual Abuse Information Network and Support) and The Clinic for Dissociative Studies. Both these organisations supported therapists who diagnosed ritual abuse, and 'survivors' who reported it. At this conference I found myself surrounded by about 180 therapists and survivors, none of whom appeared to share my scepticism, though they were aware of a 'backlash.' They had made the work of those who continued to believe in ritual abuse more difficult. Psychotherapist Valerie Sinason was spurred into developing her own clinic because the Tavistock

Clinic, where she previously held the post of child psychotherapist, declined to support further work with ritual abuse survivors. Several speakers at the conference referred to the sacrifices that were made by those who persisted in their efforts to uncover cases of ritual abuse or treat the survivors. One thing that all the publicity did not seem to have done was to change the minds of any of those who were already committed to a belief in ritual abuse.

Valerie Sinason acknowledged that believers in ritual abuse had a problem when trying to convince others of their beliefs: their knowledge of ritual abuse came solely from the testimony of alleged survivors. None had been able to provide independent, incontrovertible evidence of what had occurred. "There is a hole in the middle," she admitted. After more than a decade of searching, no relics of the reported gruesome ceremonies had been found: no bones, no bloodstains, and no bodies. There had been some successful prosecutions for child sexual abuse accompanied by strange and frightening rituals, but these did not in any way match the horrors reported by most ritual abuse survivors. Their stories always included killings, usually several of them, but there had been no prosecutions for ritual murder. She called for more research to convince others of the reality of ritual abuse, but the only method she was able to suggest was working with the survivors to provide more information on their experiences and their circumstances. This would hardly fill the hole.

Therapists at this conference had been impressed by the way their different clients told similar stories featuring cages, cannibalism, the use of bodily fluids and murder. Their clients also told of being coerced into carrying out unspeakable practices themselves so that they would be incriminated and unable to free themselves from the cult. This enabled the therapists to speak with conviction about a wide variety of cult practices and to know what to look for with new clients. A survivor told me how grateful she was that, after years of treatment with one therapist, she had gone to another one who immediately recognised the physical signs and other pointers to ritual abuse, thus enabling her to recall the details during eight more years of therapy. A history of ritual abuse was said to be hard to detect since most survivors have no conscious memories of it before going into therapy. Even when they do remember, they are said to be reluctant to tell their stories, because they are afraid both of the continuing power of the cult, and of being disbelieved by the people they turn to.

What had given the people at this conference their invincible belief in ritual abuse? In most cases it was their experience of being told "this happened to me," usually by a very disturbed and distressed individual. "No one would want to put themselves through that torment if it wasn't true," proclaimed another. "When you have eye contact with somebody you know" And "as soon as she started talking, I knew she was a survivor. When you sit in front of someone who is a genuine DID case, you cannot disbelieve." Several people spoke about the increased severity of the revelations, as their receptiveness increased. "Everything I touched seemed to escalate." Therapists themselves were often traumatised, by what the clients were telling them, and this powerful experience may have strengthened a bond in which any questioning of testimony was quite unthinkable.

Norma Howes, a social worker, and a therapist for both adults and children, told the conference that she was working with someone who did not know whether her memories were real or dreams. "Therapeutically it doesn't matter. If your dreams require metaphor of such horror, then something awful must have happened to you." She did add that you cannot use such information in the courts, because "what is compelling in therapy is not in the courts."

I had the impression that at least half of the clients seen by these therapists had DID. This was seen by itself as an indicator of severe abuse from an early age. There was much talk of how to deal with the various alters. They held important memories of the abuse, but they also served different functions, and not all of them were helpful. Some of them might be loyal to the cult which had abused them, or to their parents. Some might make allegations that were plainly ridiculous (such as being abused by aliens), and some might try to disrupt the therapy. This was attributed to 'programming' by the cult. Children were deliberately confused, so that their testimony would not be believed. Several speakers mentioned 'mind control' and the use of torture and deprivation to enslave the child and make him or her terrified of telling anybody.

Clients do not simply describe abuse and torture; they also appear to re-experience it during therapy sessions. They may scream and whimper and try to hide. They can even show bodily changes such as the spontaneous appearance of burns and wounds. Similar phenomena have been produced experimentally, using hypnosis, but the mechanism is hard to explain, and the effect is uncanny. Several therapists at the conference mentioned physical manifestations in their clients, either observed during therapy or occurring outside it. They explained these as 'body memories:' the body is remembering and re-experiencing what happened to it previously. Valerie Sinason even suggested that some unexplained physical problems occurring at the present time could be seen as evidence that earlier abuse had occurred. For example, gynaecological pain could indicate earlier sexual assault, and food allergies could be a reaction to earlier enforced cannibalism. She also claimed that full-blown DID was 'proof' of earlier torture.

The therapists who believe in ritual abuse seem to have an answer for many things that the rest of us find puzzling. Why do people who claim to be survivors of long-term ritual abuse have no memory of this before they go into therapy? The chair of RAINS, psychiatrist Dr Joan Coleman, said that RAINS accepted the reality of false memories, but thought they were less likely to be induced by therapy than by the perpetrators of ritual abuse. She pointed out that these people induced false memories deliberately, using many methods including drugs and hypnosis. These false memories were of happenings, such as alien abduction, that are so fantastic that they will discredit the testimony of the victims. Until the last session of the conference, I heard no warnings to therapists that they might unwittingly induce false memories. At this final session we were addressed by a panel of speakers including Norma Howes. She said that hypnosis must not be used to elicit memories, though it could be used in other ways to help clients. She did not elaborate on this, and her message was somewhat obscured by another panel member, a survivor, who said that she totally disagreed. "I would never have recovered my memories without hypnosis." This remark was not challenged.

I heard no dissent at this conference. Therapists and survivors shared a powerful belief system that seemed bizarre to outsiders, but which was proof against all attacks and even strengthened by the criticism it provoked. When I tentatively suggested that some aspects of survivor accounts seemed incredible, I was quickly told that some stories may be muddled because of the drugs and programming those survivors had received while in the cult, but that they are always essentially true: 'the abuse is real.' When I queried how survivors had been able to complete their education, sometimes to university level, and to function so well after a childhood of unremitting suffering, I was reminded of the wonderfully protective effect of dissociation. I did not raise the question of the lack of physical evidence of murders, tortures, and large gatherings, because I had already heard the answer: cult members had infiltrated many influential professions, and were found in the police, the legal system, parliament, and the National Health Service. Thus, prosecution could be avoided, and evidence destroyed, for example, by doctors disposing of bodies in hospital incinerators.

Believers in ritual abuse have answers for everything and can speak with impressive conviction. Sceptics, by their very nature, are doubters, who ask questions rather than give answers. I found that I could not change the views of the believers, but neither could I dismiss these people as simple-minded or crazy. The therapists I met seem to be intelligent, caring and conscientious people, genuinely wanting to relieve the suffering of their clients, while acknowledging that therapy was inevitably disturbing and that clients had to get worse before they could get better. Although no independent studies had demonstrated any benefits from this therapy, it seemed to be here to stay. Therapists and clients believed in it, and the more they engaged in it, the more their beliefs were reinforced.

Ritual abuse today

Nine years after that conference I wondered whether anything had changed. Criticism of the whole concept of ritual abuse has certainly continued, and a recent American book promoting awareness of ritual abuse, *Ritual abuse in the twenty-first century*, gives considerable space to deploring the campaigns of some sceptics. Two DID therapists have now been successfully sued by their clients for implanting false memories, and 'backlash interests' have been successful in the courts and the media in debates about ritual abuse.

In this country both the Royal College of Psychiatrists and the British Psychological Society have issued guidelines for their members, warning them of the unreliability of memory, and the difficulties faced by therapists in dealing with past events. The British Psychological Society warns that "it is not really possible to establish whether a memory represents factual events without external corroboration" and advises that:

> Psychologists should avoid being drawn into a search for memories of abuse. Psychologists should avoid engaging in activities and techniques which are intended to reveal indications of past sexual abuse of which the client has no memory (British Psychological Society, 2000).

Many clients would have been spared the distress of believing that they had been ritually abused if only their therapists had followed this advice. My impression is that clinical psychologists working in the NHS are now more aware of the dangers of promoting false memories and are far less likely to diagnose DID or discover ritual abuse. Sadly, however, there is now a growing band of independent therapists who work privately and are unlikely to ever see any guidelines. It seemed to me that at the 2001 RAINS conference, nearly all the therapists were in private practice, often with no recognised training or supervision.

In 2009 RAINS, in conjunction with an organisation called Trauma and Abuse Group (TAG), held a further conference. I attended this and discovered that little had changed in the previous eight years. This time there were approximately 200 delegates; most of them were therapists or counsellors, working for small, independent organisations. Many said that they were new to this kind of work and spoke of their amazement at encountering dissociated personalities and of their horror at hearing their disclosures. I also met people who identified themselves as survivors of ritual abuse. Some had been in therapy for many years, but some had moved on and were now themselves offering therapy to other survivors. Several had written books about their experiences. Once again there was an air of excitement about the demanding work of uncovering horrors. "We are all pioneers," declared one of the speakers, a Canadian psychologist. "This is cutting edge therapy, not the Mickey Mouse theory you hear about at graduate school."

All the speakers at the conference were in private practice and spoke authoritatively about the continued reality of ritual abuse. The continuing lack of any external evidence for this did not seem to discourage them. Reference was briefly made to setbacks, especially in the United States, from sceptics who had successfully sued therapists and stopped some people from coming forward. However, delegates were simply told to avoid getting caught up in 'the false memory controversy,' and were reassured that the tide was now turning. I reluctantly felt that this could well be true. I was as impressed as I had been in 2001, by the dedication and uncritical enthusiasm of both delegates and speakers, and by the support that they provided for each other in exploring their nightmarish worlds. Awareness of external criticism had simply driven these believers into each other's arms and away from all the restraining influences.

The detection of ritual abuse and the treatment of its 'survivors' now seems to be mainly restricted to the unregulated fringes of therapeutic activity. This can make it even more dangerous. Seemingly magical therapies are flourishing all around us. They often engender a placebo effect of well-being, and many people are happy to try remedies without questioning where they came from or how they are supposed to work. One can only hope that these people will be wary of any self-styled counsellor or healer who claims to understand the strange phenomenon of dissociation. If anything in their behaviour leads their therapist into diagnosing DID, they in turn will be led into a complete rewriting of their personal history. Major life changes may follow, as ties with families and friends are severed. Those who previously supported them may now be seen, at best, as unhelpful disbelievers, at worst, as members of a murderess cult.

With prolonged therapy (and it usually is prolonged) the break can be very far reaching. A 'Christian counsellor' reported:

What Laura and I only discovered years later, from her other personalities, was that neighbours were involved in the ritual group, as were teachers at her school, and the family doctor, so that those whom Laura thought as a child might offer her safety were perpetrators too (Cooke, 2008).

Poor Laura! She now has only her therapist for support.

References:

Cooke, S. Opening Pandora's Box. In Sachs, A. & Galton, G. (eds.). *Forensic aspects of dissociative identity disorder.* Karmac, London (2008), pp. 155 – 166.

Merskey, H. The manufacture of personalities: the production of multiple personality disorder. *British Journal of Psychiatry* (1992), pp. 327 – 340.

Miller, A. Recognising and treating survivors of abuse by organised criminal gangs. In Noblitt, R., & Noblitt, P. P. (eds.), *Ritual Abuse in the twenty-first century: psychological, forensic, social and political considerations.* Robert D. Reed (2008), Ch. 3.

Ross, C. a., Epidemiology of multiple personality disorder and dissociation. *Psychiatric Clinics of North America.* (1991), pp. 503 – 517.

Rutz, C., Becker, T., Overcamp, B. & Karriker, W. Exploring commonalities reported by adult survivors of extreme abuse: preliminary empirical findings. In Noblitt, R., & Noblitt, P. P. (eds.), *Ritual Abuse in the twenty-first century: psychological, forensic, social, and political considerations.* Robert D. Reed (2008), Ch. 3.

Schreiber, F. R., *Sybil.* Regnery, Chicago (1973).

Smith, M. & Padzer, L. *Michelle Remembers.* Congdon & Lattes. New York (1980).

Victor, J. S, *Satanic panic: the creation of a contemporary legend*, Open Court. Chicago (1993).

Waterhouse, R., Satanic cults: how the hysteria swept Britain. *The Independent on Sunday*, 16 September (1990), p. 3.

Noblitt, R & Noblitt, P. P. Redefining the language of ritual abuse and the politics that dictate it. In Noblitt, R., & Noblitt, P. P. (eds.), *Ritual Abuse in the twenty-first century: psychological, forensic, social, and political considerations*, Ch. 2. Robert D. Reed (2008).

THE CAROL FELSTEAD SCANDAL

The Carol Myers/Felstead case is discussed in detail in Justice for Carol – the creation of a Satanic myth in the United Kingdom (Felstead and Felstead, Create Space Independent Publishing Platform, 2014). The blurb to Justice for Carol read as follows:

Justice for Carol is a groundbreaking and devastating personal account of the heartbreak inflicted onto a hitherto normal family after Carol was incorrectly diagnosed as a victim of Satanic Ritual Abuse.

Carol was hypnotised, sedated, and brainwashed. Her childhood memories were eradicated, and her mind was reordered. Carol was assigned a new identity, separated from her family, and a myth was created which helped stoke the entire Satanic Abuse panic in the United Kingdom.

Out of the blue, in 2005, Carol phoned her brother and said she wanted to return home. One week later she died in mysterious circumstances.

We then embarked on a quest to discover the truth about Carol's life and death. Caught in a frightening conspiracy of silence, misinformation, and institutional cover ups, we discovered what had really happened to destroy her body and soul.

The following narrative utilises Carol's voluminous medical and psychiatric records, police investigations initiated by the Felstead family, inquest transcripts, a high court judgement, and detailed correspondence with the attorney general's office. As I wrote in Justice for Carol (JFC), "this is a story that many will find incredible, but nevertheless it is true." The opening passages in this chapter are extracted from JFC, and document contemporaneous conversations as events unfolded in 2005. The following chapter begins where JFC concluded. It is important this scandal is not erased from history for it represents an extreme example of the dangers of RMT which has befallen thousands of families in the UK and millions of families worldwide.

By Dr Kevin Felstead

14 July 2005 – The Coroner's Officer

"Hello. My name is Sharon Marshall. I am a Coroner's Officer, based in Battersea Coroner's Office. Am I speaking to Richard?"

"Yes."

"I'm very sorry to tell you but Carol has died."
"When did she die?"

Sharon Marshall replied:
"We're not sure yet, but we're saying it was the 29th of June, as that was the day she was found."

The date was particularly poignant to Richard, because, on that very day, he had written a letter to Carol, giving her an outline of what the family had been doing, and providing a copy of his email address, as another potential channel of communication. Sharon Marshall explained:

"We were told there was no family. I got your contact details from the letter you wrote to Carol – I don't know why the police held onto it for the past two weeks. I've only come across it on my desk just now."

"What did she die of?" asked Richard.

"We're still awaiting the results of laboratory tests. Do you want me to call back later when it might be easier for you?"

Richard experienced a helpless feeling as he listened to the Coroner's Officer's words.

She continued:

"I've spoken to the next of kin and she's arranged the funeral for tomorrow. Lots of Carol's friends are taking time off work so they can attend and the next of kin has said you're welcome to attend."

The call ended with Sharon Marshall promising to telephone back. Richard immediately entered the next room where our brother, David, was working at his laptop. Without pausing he blurted out:

"Carol's dead!"

David let out a sigh – instinctively moving his left hand to his forehead as David leaned back in his chair. Tears filled his eyes, and he asked in a sombre tone of voice: "When did she die?"

"They are not certain", Richard replied, "but her body was found on the 29th of June."

Carol had been estranged from our family; however, it had been previously arranged during the past few weeks that either Carol would drive to Stockport to visit David and Richard, or, alternatively, they would visit London to meet her. Both shared the same feeling of complete and utter defeat – as death had cheated them of meeting Carol ever again.

The 'next of kin'

David barely had time to digest the news when the telephone rang again. Richard assumed the Coroner's Officer had forgotten to ask some important questions which urgently required his response. He rushed back into the front room and picked up the 'phone.

"Oh Hello," am I speaking to Richard?" asked a woman, whose voice he did not recognise.

"Yes."

"I'm Carol's next of kin. Since I know you're not one of the family who harmed Carol, I thought you might like to come to the funeral we're having for her tomorrow."

 "Who are you?"

"That's not important at the moment."
"What did she die of?"

"Carol had a very difficult childhood," responded the anonymous caller.

"What do you mean she had a very difficult childhood?" Richard said emphatically, "She did not."

 Of all the people in the family Richard was the one who had been closest to Carol during her early youth, and he knew that her childhood had been for the most part ordinary and uneventful – that is, uneventful in the sense of being happy and normal.

"Who are you?"

"I'm Carol's friend. I knew her for 20 years. Carol was ill for a long time and received a lot of medical treatment. I used to check up on Carol two or three times a week. I spoke to Carol the Sunday before she died – she was feeling unwell. She had a doctor's appointment on Monday which she had to cancel. I rang her on Wednesday but there was no answer, so I called her doctor."

She then explained how the doctor had alerted police and how they had gone round to the flat – and that was where they found her lifeless body.

How did Carol die?

"She had a very difficult childhood."
"What was the exact medical diagnosis?"
The caller sighed again repeating the same statement. "Carol had a very difficult childhood."
The woman switched tack and began talking about the funeral planned for the following day. The caller let go of the previous exasperation she'd expressed and started enthusiastically describing the preparations that had been made: the large number of Carol's friends who would be taking time off work to attend – hundreds of mourners, not only from London but from across the entire country – and she reiterated how Richard was welcome to attend.

Richard knew he couldn't possibly decide about attending Carol's funeral without speaking to the other members of his family. It seemed to him such an obvious position to adopt that he didn't even bother stating it to the caller. Conversely, he went back to the questions he'd already asked, repeating them in different forms to try and elicit a response that would clarify the identity of the caller and the cause of Carol's death, but no matter how he approached the subjects the caller gave the same answers every time, to the point where her robotic replies seemed to be indicative of either mental aberration or malicious intent.

The conversation went back and forth, with every attempt to ascertain the caller's identity, what had happened to Carol, and why she died, stonewalled each time. Finally, the anonymous caller slammed down the phone.

A few minutes later, the phone rang again. It was the Coroner's Officer. She asked:

"Is that Richard?"

"Yes."
"Where was Carol born?"
"Stockport," answered Richard, surprised by the question.
Sharon Marshall paused for a moment, as though the reply was significant, and repeated the question, "*Where* was Carol born?"
"Stockport," he reiterated.
Sharon Marshall asked: "When was the last time you spoke to Carol?"
"I spoke to Carol on the 20th and 21st June, last month."

Richard then described the contents of the first two-minute conversation with his sister, in which Carol said she was ill, was out of work, but wanted to move back to Stockport to be with her family because she was lonely and had no friends in London. He recalled that initially her speech was a serious cause for concern, as she was slurring her words. Richard explained that Carol sounded as if she was medicated.

Carol then said she would visit Richard and David the following week, by driving from London to Stockport, providing she had the money (Carol said she was 'broke'). Richard suggested that, if there was a problem, then David and he would drive to London to visit her. Richard asked for her current address, which she provided. Richard also said he'd write a letter so that Carol had his contact details – including email, which she could use as a free means of communication. There was a brief discussion about Richard's business and personal life, to which he responded briefly and asked the same questions of Carol. There was a truly profound longing in her voice, and a desire to say something she didn't enunciate which was unforgettable. Carol said she'd telephone Richard the next day.

Carol did telephone the next day. To his relief she sounded much better – which confirmed to Richard in his own mind that she had been on medication the previous day – and Carol was much more optimistic in her outlook.

Sharon Marshall listened and seemed to be noting down what Richard said. He asked again about the date and cause of death. She responded: "We don't know the date of death, but we're saying it was 29 June, as that was when she was found. There's going to be an inquest."

Marshall then addressed the issue of the funeral and said that all the arrangements had been made, lots of Carol's friends were attending, and they'd gone to a lot of trouble to take the time off work. Several hundred people were attending from London and across the country. These words were surprising to Richard – because the coroner's officer used almost identical words to those spoken by the anonymous caller a few minutes ago.

Richard was vague about attending the funeral – his parents needed to be informed of Carol's death. Such a rush and he was still in a state of shock.

"I need to speak to my father before making any decision."

15 July 2005

Richard made a written record of the various telephone conversations, assuming in the light of the coroner's process and the forthcoming inquest that we would need to call on them subsequently. He did not know that he would be starting a process that would last for 19 years. After Richard had spoken with Sharon Marshall for the final time, he passed her contact details to my father. The following day Dad telephoned her.

He introduced himself and she said: "I've spoken to your son, Richard. You do know your daughter's died?"

"Yes," he said succinctly.

Marshall repeated the question she asked Richard the previous day.

"Can you verify where your daughter was born?"

"Stockport," he replied.

She paused, and then said: "Are you sure?"

"Yes."

"Do you know that Carol made a number of allegations about the family?"

"Why would Carol do that?"

My father didn't understand what she meant, and he tried to clarify her words.

"What allegations?" he responded, perplexed.

"Carol said she had been abused."

Dad was shocked by this statement – in fact, he was totally taken aback. He tried to remain composed.

"She said that?" Has Carol been ill?" Then he used a word he never used in ordinary life. "Has she been sectioned?"

"Yes."

Dad hesitated pondering whether this was a case of mistaken identity.

"The person you're describing doesn't sound like the daughter I know."

Sharon Marshall continued tentatively.

"Do you know Carol changed her name?"

"No. Why would she do that? What is her new name?"

"Carol Myers."

Carol's previous surname was 'Felstead.'

He repeated himself.

"That doesn't sound like the daughter I know."

"There have been allegations of grandparental abuse."

My father was appalled by this false claim. He paused for a moment: this grotesque allegation was difficult to comprehend.

"There *was* the court case," she added quietly.

Dad's puzzlement increased even more.

"Court case? What court case?" he asked.

"The court case that took place in Manchester and collapsed after 3 days – due to lack of evidence."

Dad was bewildered.

"Who was in that then?"

He was wondering whether Carol had been involved in some sort of incident and had taken the perpetrators to trial. Dad had no idea that the alleged criminals were supposed to be us. But the inference was clear: members of our family were meant to have been involved in the trial and Carol was supposed to have been the complainant.

Marshall appeared genuinely surprised at his response and seemed not to know what to say next.

"Your daughter left a Life Assessment. It's very upsetting."

Dad was thinking to himself: a 'Life Assessment? Why would she leave a Life Assessment?'

Dad asked Sharon Marshall, what had happened to Carol's possessions? – the coroner's officer appeared to know only about Carol's computer, which she said had been given away to a Salvation Army charity shop.

The conversation swiftly lost impetus and the telephone call quickly came to an end.

My father is a pragmatic person, who is generally slow to anger. He brooded on the recent course of events and then made up his mind what he was going to do. It was now clear that the Coroner's Officer had been supplied with false information about Carol's life and about an imaginary trial that had not taken place.

When he finally spoke to her for the second time, Dad thought that she was quiet, to the point of being subdued.

My father questioned Marshall about the claims Carol was supposed to have made and what exactly she had been told had happened to Carol. The story she related was both horrifying and preposterous. The allegations were based on the mysterious 'Life Assessment,' which we later discovered the unknown 'next of kin' had passed to the coroner and to the police. When we were sent a copy (in August 2005), the six-page document was not dated. It was not signed. It did not contain specific names or any information which identified that it had been written by Carol. On the first page, someone had scribbled in black ink (not in Carol's handwriting) that the document was written while Carol was in a psychiatric hospital, some years earlier. It stated that Carol was born in Manchester, and the 'Life Assessment', on which Sharon Marshall attached considerable credence, claimed Carol had been abused from the moment she was born, had been mute from the age of five, and was unable to complete her schooling. My mother was supposed to have murdered another daughter, placed the dead baby on top of Carol, and then burned the house to the ground – presumably to conceal what she had done. Carol was allegedly starved throughout her childhood but managed somehow to become a nurse and, later, to free herself from the clutches of our family (who were meant to be the leaders of a Satanic Cult) by prosecuting my parents at a trial in Manchester, which was supposed to have occurred after she left home sometime in the late 1980s. The trial, Sharon Marshall alleged, collapsed after three days due to lack of evidence. When my family read the document, we recognised it as being so full of ridiculous fantasies and lies, we were amazed that *anyone* could give it credibility.

Every single claim in this document was false. The spectacularly ludicrous accusation that my mother murdered her own daughter and burned down the house while Carol was still alive was demonstrably impossible. Mum and Dad had a daughter who died a medically documented death inside the walls of our local hospital. Joan Julie was born and died in 1962. The house fire did happen, but it was a tragic accident which was reported on the front page of our local newspaper on 28 November 1963 (we were made homeless and given temporary accommodation in a hostel).

TRAPPED IN BLAZE

Three terrified baby boys were trapped upstairs in a blazing house on Tuesday while their hysterical mother beat frantically with her fists on the locked back door screaming for help.

All three were rescued from the choking fumes with only seconds to spare as fire swept through the terraced house. First indication of the fire came when neighbours heard frenzied screaming. They rushed from their back doors and saw 22-yeard-old Mrs Joan Felstead banging at her back door and screaming: "My children, my children. Someone get my children out; the house is on fire."

Fireman arrived after minutes and although only one was wearing breathing apparatus, four managed to grope their way through the front room. The house was severely damaged. Fire Chief Harrison said the downstairs room was like an inferno when he arrived.

Later the three boys and their mother were taken to hospital and treated for shock and the effects of smoke.

With the three children – Kevin, three, and twins David and Anthony, two, sitting beside her, Mrs Felstead explained what happened:

"This has been a terrible year," she said. "I have lost two children already during the past 12 months. I've got nothing left now – only my family."

The second deceased child, Christopher, was stillborn in 1963. Carol was born in 1964. Therefore, she wasn't alive when these events took place. Moreover, they were not deemed suspicious; there was no question of police involvement at any time.

The 2005 Inquest

The inquest into Carol's death took place on 12 August 2005. For those unacquainted with the procedures of a coroner's court, there may be numerous short inquests held during a single day. My family sat in a side room waiting for proceedings to commence prior to being approached by Sharon Marshall. She appeared age-wise to be in her mid-thirties. Of slim build with dark hair and smart business-like appearance, she was well spoken and articulate. Her manner was polite, officious, and friendly, though restrained. Minor pleasantries were exchanged, although my father repeated some of the things he said to her previously on the telephone, reiterating that Carol had a normal and loving upbringing. We had previously posted a large envelope of photographs to the Coroner's Office – photographs which by their very normality disproved the ludicrous fantasies disseminated about Carol's life. There was no mention of the 'next of kin.' My father would say later, "we were given no explanation about her absence, which, on that day, seemed incomprehensible." He asked Ms Marshall to show the photographs to Carol's psychiatrist to demonstrate that Carol had lived an entirely ordinary life, and had not been malnourished, friendless and neglected as had been claimed. The photographs covered the entire period from early childhood up to the age of 21, before Carol left home. They showed her smiling in every image, on her own, and with friends at school and on holiday. Sharon Marshall later acknowledged that Dr I had seen the photographs.

"What did she say?" asked Dad.

"She said, Oh Dear!"

Dad was astonished and interpreted those words as being an admission that the psychiatrist had been provided a false history about Carol's life and had only now realised that the false accusations were untenable.

Since we had already disproven their existence, there was no legitimate reason why the fantastical accusations should be raised. My father was quite prepared to stop the inquest if an attempt to pervert the course of justice was made, and to instigate prosecution of anyone who should give false evidence claiming it to be fact.

"Please rise for Her Majesty's Coroner."

Dr Shirley Radcliffe (Deputy Coroner) opened the inquest.

"Now this in an inquest into the death of Carol Myers. Miss Marshall if you'd like to help with identification."

Sharon Marshall responded inaudibly. It was difficult to hear what she said, and she appeared to be nervous.

Coroner:

"You have an identification."

Marshall:

"I do ma'am. On Tuesday 12 July 2005, the deceased was identified as Carol Myers, aged 41 years born on 8 June 1964 in Stockport."

There were insurmountable problems with this introductory statement. On the surface it appears to be quite convincing, but upon a deeper analysis it is clearly misleading. As Carol's funeral was arranged by the 'next of kin' for 15 July, it requires a leap of faith to accept that identification took place three days previously. It is necessary to register a death and to then provide a death certificate for a funeral director and funeral services for obvious reasons need be paid for in advance. The truth is that Carol's identity had been known from the moment she had died.

Coroner:

"Do you have some background information."

Sharon Marshall then read out our family statement.

"We have given Carol a family burial and she will always be in our hearts and will be remembered as a loving, kind, caring daughter, and sister. With love, Mum, Dad, and the family."

Police testified that officers had forced entry into Carol's flat on Wednesday 29 June 2005.

Coroner:

"A friend had contacted her friend's doctor as she was concerned for her friend, Carol Myers, and the police had been informed of this and you arrived on the scene and tried ringing and knocking with no response."

The "friend" was the "next of kin." Her name was Dr Fleur Fisher. She was a former head of ethics at the British Medical Association (BMA). The BMA is a trade union and professional body for doctors in the UK. According to its website, "the medical ethics committee debates ethical issues on the relationship between the medical profession, the public and the state."

Dr Fisher was not named or called to give evidence at the inquest. We now know that on the day of Carol's death she made an emergency 999 telephone call to police allegedly from Manchester expressing her concern that Carol had taken her own life. The emergency telephone call was not mentioned during the inquest.

Police described how they forced entry into Carol's flat which was in a state of disarray. Clothes and bed linen were scattered around the bedroom. Extensive medication was strewn across a bedside cabinet and floor. She was naked from the waist down. White foam ran either side of her face, and orange liquid was present on the bedside table. The liquid was not subjected to laboratory tests. Carol was cyanosed indicating that she had been dead for some time.

Carol's psychiatrist testified that Carol had been diagnosed with a borderline personality disorder for which she had been prescribed extensive anti-psychotic medication. She had taken three overdoses and was under the care of the Community Mental Health Team. Carol had received extensive psychotherapy and psychiatric treatment.

A cause of death was indeterminable. Carol may have suffered from an electrolyte imbalance which may have led to a cardia arrhythmia. But that was far from certain. The coroner recorded an Open Verdict.

It was not until we obtained the inquest transcript several months later that glaring anomalies became apparent. "If we knew then what we know now, we would have had the inquest in uproar," said Dad. "They took advantage of our ignorance."

Carol's Medical Records

On a cold winter morning in 2007, my father was walking past his old medical practice. A few days previously, we had discussed the difficulty of gaining access to Carol's medical records, and pondered how it may be possible to obtain them. Dad walked into the building. It was lunchtime and the reception area was ghostly quiet. He spoke with the receptionist.

"I don't suppose you can help me," he began tentatively. "My name is Joseph Felstead, and this used to be my doctor's – I was a patient here about eight years ago."

The receptionist looked up from the desk and listened attentively.

"My daughter was also a patient here in the 1980s. The problem I've got is – my daughter died two years ago, and her doctor won't allow me to see her notes, which she said remain confidential even though she has died. Are old medical records kept on the premises?"

She quickly grasped the situation and replied:

"We don't keep medical records here. Once a patient dies, the records are temporarily stored with the Primary Care Trust, before being sent on to the Primary Care Support Service. To gain access you will need to provide proof of identity and then the records should be released to you."

Rather than waste any time, as soon as he got home my father telephoned the Primary Care Support Service who confirmed what he had been told. However, in addition to providing proof of identity, Dad would also need to provide Letters of Administration and a detailed covering letter. A Medical

Assessor would then evaluate the documentation. Recognising its importance, the family prepared an extensive covering letter. While we did not regard it as a forgone conclusion, we were confident of the overwhelming logic of our case. Sure enough, in May 2008, Carol's records were eventually released to us and, finally, we now had the opportunity to uncover Carol's medical and psychiatric history.

Even so, because the records were incomplete, several protracted enquiries were to follow. In 2010 and 2012, two sets of Carol's psychiatric records – amounting to several thousand pages – were obtained following an arduous struggle. These notes have been conflated to provide an overview of Carol's treatment. The first point to make is that Carol's medical records for the first 16 years are missing almost in their entirety. We know they existed because there are references to them in a solicitor's letter from the mid-1990s when Carol was considering initiating legal action after she injured herself following a fall in a rehabilitation centre in 1993. It is extraordinary that there are no medical records whatsoever for Carol's formative years when she was fit and healthy. Moreover, the files contain only a handful of letters written in the mid and late 1980s. If we are to set these aside, we can say that in effect the records pertaining to the first 26 years of Carol's life are missing.

The documents in Carol's medical file that have survived show that she complained to her doctor about persistent headaches. One consultant wrote: "there is no family history of any significance;" another consultant gave her "a clean bill of health." A third commented that, "her headaches could well represent migraine but may well be associated with the recent tension in the run up to her (nursing) finals."

A letter dated 10 November 1986 illustrates that Carol was later referred by occupational health to the psychology department where she received recovered memory therapy, using hypnosis.

We now had an explanation as to why Carol had drifted away from our family in the 1980s – she was effectively being brainwashed. Following hypnosis, Carol would come to believe that she was a victim of SRA. She would claim that the abuse started age two – three years, but she did not recall it until her early twenties. Carol's medical notes reveal that she was later given a form of experimental hypnosis known as autogenic training by Vera Diamond, an untrained psychotherapist, at her Harley Street clinic in London. This 'treatment' was supported by vast amounts of psychotropic medication. A few years later a psychiatrist asserted: "I think it is possible that Carol does not actually remember very much about it. Vera Diamond's approach was based on a form of hypnosis about which she may not have a great deal of recollection."

Carol received RMT from Valerie Sinason at the Tavistock Clinic in London. Her treatment involved five-hour weekly sessions beginning in October 1992 concluding in May 1993. Sinason described Carol as "her first chronic sadistic-abuse patient." The myth of SRA in the UK was built around Carol's recovered memories. In interview (published as a seven- page feature in the *Observer Magazine* in December 2011) with journalist Will Storr, Sinason described her first appointment with Carol who was limping.

"I just had that nasty feeling," she says. "It's her, and she's been hurt by them."

Will Storr:

"You could tell that from the limp?"

"Yep."

Will Storr:

"Soon, we get to the actual Satanism. Sinason talks of a popular ritual in which a child is stitched inside the belly of a dying animal before being reborn to Satan. During other celebrations, people eat faeces, menstrual blood, semen, urine. There's cannibalism. Some groups have doctors performing abortions. They give the foetus to the mother, and she's made to kill the baby."

Carol's psychiatric records are littered with bizarre claims about sacrificial slaughter, rape, infanticide, and ritual murder. The serial killer, Harold Shipman was meant to have been a member of the cult. One reference in Carol's notes, said that Carol was reborn ritually out of a bull's stomach, placed in a grave "on top of her dead sister" and rescued by my father who was supposed to have been dressed as the devil. Following therapy, Carol would claim to have given birth to six children who were supposedly conceived by cult members, "aborted and ritually sacrificed." Dr Fisher planted a rose tree in memory of the fictitious children.

The Life assessment document

Every single statement made in this six-page 'report' is fantastical and demonstrably false. For the sake of brevity, it is summarised in the passages below.

I grew up in constant fear and terror of endangerment of my life. At three years of age, my mother smothered my sister who was born with Down's Syndrome; she sat me on top of her and set fire to the house. I convinced myself that I had killed her and was responsible for her death. It was around this time that I first recall being Satanically Abused. The shock of stumbling upon the gowns that they wore left me mute until the age of five.

I felt trapped, everyone I knew was involved – I had no escape route, nowhere to turn, nowhere to hide. The abuse continued in a ritualistic way and occurred mainly on religious days. It involved snuff films, drugs, prostitution, and alcohol; and went on until my late twenties.

As the abuse became more 'organised' many professionals became perpetrators, and I became fearful. I cut of all contact with my family but wherever I worked or moved to, they would follow me and threaten to kill me if I spoke to anyone about the abuse.

The exploitative introduction of Joan Julie who died in hospital, in 1962, before Carol was born, under the auspices of medical staff, remains sickening to this day. These false allegations, which were not subjected to the slightest critical scrutiny by any of the authorities, were treated with deadly seriousness by the coroner's officer following Carol's death in June 2005. If that wasn't the case, then Sharon Marshall would not have raised the life assessment.

Dr Fisher and RMT

In 1986, Carol received counselling from Dr Fisher. Her interview with journalist Will Storr is instructive.

From the telephone interview:

Will Storr:

"Is that Dr Fisher?"

Dr Fisher:

"Yes."

Will Storr:

"I tell her that I want to talk about Carol."

Dr Fisher:

"I'm leery about putting my head above the parapet on that subject. And if you don't mind me saying so, it's not wise for you to be involving yourself in this story either. That family, they're bloody terrifying."

Will Storr:

"You're frightened of them?"

Dr Fisher:

"Of course, I'm frightened. They're frightening people. And the things they've been saying about me, she says, adding confusingly, I'm not a psychiatrist! I'm not a therapist."

Dr Fisher initially denied that she gave Carol RMT.

Will Storr:

"I have the letter here and it is dated 27 November 1986, and it says: "She required to see Dr Fisher for psychosexual counselling."

Dr Fisher:

"Psychosexual is the wrong term."

Will Storr:

"What's the correct term?"

Dr Fisher:

"Uh, I really don't know. People come and tell you things that have happened to them."

Will Storr:

There is a silence.

"Things like abuse?"

Dr Fisher:

"Things that have happened to them," she repeats crossly. "I'm not saying anything else. It's not right that this woman's privacy should be breached in this way." She is shouting now. "She's dead! She's goddamned dead!"

Will Storr:

"Were you ever worried that Carol had lapsed into fantasy?"

Dr Fisher:

"Never," she says.

Will Storr:

"By 1997, I tell her, Carol was claiming that a former Conservative cabinet minister had anally raped her with a claw hammer in Conservative central office."

Will Storr:

"For a moment she doesn't speak."

Dr Fisher:

"That's not something I knew about. It may have been fantasy," she says, adding darkly, "but I couldn't say."

Will Storr:

"Are you aware of any evidence that any of Carol's claims actually happened?"

Dr Fisher:

"I never looked for any evidence."

Will Storr:

"Then what made you believe her?"

Dr Fisher:

"She's not the only patient I've had who told the same kind of stories."

Will Storr:

"About ritual abuse?"

Dr Fisher:

"It turned out to be that, yes. The people didn't remember at first. They weren't aware. They were memories they'd had a long time, and they just came out."

In a separate interview with investigative journalist Daniel Foggo, Dr Fisher admitted that Carol had "no knowledge" of being ritually abused when she first treated her. "Very often," she said, "people who have had difficult experiences repress them then they suddenly begin to come back in dreams or flashbacks."

Our complaints to the metropolitan police service and general medical council.

Following the 2005 inquest, we reflected further on Carol's life and premature death before instigating several protracted – and exhaustive – enquiries. Perhaps of most significance were our complaints to the general medical council and to the metropolitan police service. The latter investigated Dr Fisher for theft of Carol's possessions and for attempting to arrange an illegal cremation service. As a senior coroner would write subsequently:

The Felstead family discovered that it was Dr Fisher who contacted the police on the day of Ms Myers being found dead. They also found out that, following Ms Myers death, Dr Fisher took steps to transfer the insurance to Ms Myers' car to herself and to sell the contents of Ms Myers' flat. Dr Fisher offered explanations for these matters, but the Felstead family have not accepted these explanations.

That is a significant understatement: we have emphatically rejected the 'explanations' robustly and repeatedly.

The coroner also confirmed that in 2005 Dr Fisher had completed cremation forms, prior to Richard being informed of Carol's death. From our perspective, our police complaint was an open and shut case. Yet, following a 15-month investigation into Dr Fisher, Detective M wrote:

The reviewing lawyer states that it will be difficult to prove that Dr Fisher acted otherwise than in good faith and with sincerity when she disposed of Carol's things and when she assumed responsibility for the cremation arrangements.

The reviewing lawyer for the crown prosecution service added:

It may have been that since 1985 Dr Fisher may have acted in a way that influenced or encouraged Carol's behaviour (separation from the family) and resulting in Carol repeating allegations which set off a spiral of mental health diagnoses.

That is also a significant understatement. As I wrote in *Justice for Carol*, "Though she was 41 when she died, the truth is that her life ended at 21 when she went to see her doctor about a headache."

The General Medical Council responded to our complaint as follows:

Thank you for your letter of 26 March 2010 regarding the Police investigation into the death of your sister.

The case examiners reviewed the information and decided to conclude your case with no action. In doing so they gave their reasons as follows:

Dr Fisher, a 73-year-old doctor who retired from active clinical practice, first came to the GMCs attention following an enquiry from the Metropolitan Police who were investigating her for alleged dishonesty, theft and attempting to arrange an illegal cremation of the body of Ms Myers.

These are serious allegations that could affect the doctor's registration.

According to police documents, Ms Myers died in June 2005. It appears that Dr Fisher helped to dispose of Ms Myers possessions and wanted to arrange for her body to be cremated. However, the Coroner's Officer released her body to Ms Myers family to arrange for a funeral to take place.

A family member appears to have complained subsequently that Dr Fisher may have been inappropriately attempting to keep Carol's death from them, and that she inappropriately attempted to arrange a cremation without their knowledge.

The Police have provided the GMC with a copy of their interview with Dr Fisher (from April 2008). From this it appears that Dr Fisher treated Ms Myers in 1985/6 but only for a short while before her care was taken over by others.

The Police have closed their case with no further action.

There is insufficient evidence to support the allegations and no realistic prospect of establishing Dr Fisher's fitness to practise is impaired to a degree justifying action against her. The case can be closed.

The investigatory bodies did not find sufficient concern to act against Dr Fisher who was operating in plain sight. We think that their decisions are appalling.

Application to overturn the 2005 Inquest

In 2015, I made complaints about Valerie Sinason to the British Psychoanalytic Council (BPS) and to the Association of Child Psychotherapists (ACP). The former determined that our complaint ought to be put on hold pending the outcome of the ACP complaint. The latter complaint dragged on, and on, and on. It felt like pulling teeth. Ultimately, Dr Sinason was subjected to a disciplinary hearing, which culminated in fresh allegations against us, and concluded that she had not breached ethical guidelines.

We obtained audio and written transcripts of the inquest. It was riddled with so many errors and omissions that my brother suggested drafting an application to the Attorney General's Office to seek permission for referral to the High Court to quash the 2005 inquest. The application was referred to the Solicitor General who gave rare permission (*Fiat*) to apply to the High Court.

On 19 December 2014 we were listed for a hearing in the High Court, based in the Royal Courts of Justice (RCJ). This was a significant development. The RCJ comprises of three different divisions and incorporates the civil and criminal courts of appeal. Located on the Strand in London 'it is reminiscent of a cathedral in both style and scale. Soaring arches and beautifully stained-glass windows, ornamented with the coats of arms of Lord Chancellors and keepers of the Great Seal, combined with a mosaic marble floor leading to a maze of enchanting corridors to create a majestic setting.'

The presiding judges were Mr Justice Ouseley and His Honour Judge Peter Thornton (then the senior coroner for England and Wales) QC. The following passages appear in their original form in a verbal and written judgement handed out on the day, which neatly encapsulated our concerns about the 2005 inquest.

High Court Judgement

MR JUSTICE OUSELEY:

This is an application brought by David Felstead, the brother of Carol Patricia Myers, with the fiat of the Solicitor General, dated 4 March 2014. The applicant seeks an order under section 13(1)(b) of the Coroner's Act 1988 (as amended) to quash the inquisition into the death of Ms Myers and to direct that a fresh inquest be heard. The applicant now seeks a fresh inquest into his sister's death. He puts forward a number of grounds, the first of which is presented on the basis of "the discovery of new facts or evidence," one of the bases upon which it may be just to hold a new inquest pursuant to section 13(1)(b).

The principal point concerns a Dr Fleur Fisher, a former clinician who had years before treated Ms Myers. She had described herself as the 'next of kin' of Ms Myers and 'executor' of her estate. Dr Fisher was not called to give evidence at the inquest.

The point arises in this way. At around the time of death of Ms Myers, it was Dr Fisher who made the 999-emergency call, at 3. 14 pm. In this significant call, she told the police that she was a friend of Ms Myers, and had serious concerns for her welfare, and that she might have taken a drug overdose. Dr Fisher added that she had been unable to reach Ms Myers by telephone and that Ms Myers would be in the bedroom at the rear of Ms Myers' property. It was as a result of this call that the police went to the flat and forced entry. At the time of the inquest, this 999 call was said by a police witness to have been made by a "friend" of Ms Myers, as she was concerned for her friend. No mention was made at the inquest of Dr Fisher.

Subsequent to the inquest, enquiries by the family revealed that this call had, indeed, been made by Dr Fisher. Enquiries to the coroner also revealed a letter from the coroner dated 10 October 2006 that this "initial informant" had described herself to the coroner's officer as the "next of kin," stating there was no family to contact. Dr Fisher also provided a photograph for the coroner for identification purposes.

In addition, the "friend", Dr Fisher, had provided to the coroner's officer a document (allegedly written by Ms Myers) in which she claimed she had been sexually abused as a child, referring to ritual satanic abuse both by her family and others. The document was subsequently given by the coroner to the family. Dr Fisher also made arrangements for cremation.

In my judgement, some of this is potentially material evidence, which, if available at the time of the inquest could have made a difference to the coroner's decision. At the very least there should have been, and now can be, enquiry into the reasons for the 999-phone call by Dr Fisher, and whether she knew or suspected that Ms Myers may have taken an overdose and, if so, why? There should be exploration of what Dr Fisher knew about the deceased's health and state of mind shortly before her death, and of her behaviour. She may have been the last person to have contact with Ms Myers before her death. I am therefore satisfied, as a result of new facts and evidence, that it is necessary and desirable in the interests of justice under section 13 (1) of the Coroner's Act 1988 (as amended) that another inquest should be held.

Accordingly, if HHJ Thornton agrees, under section 13(1)(2) the inquisition taken on 12 August 2005 will be quashed, and a fresh investigation will be ordered (including an inquest to be held into the death by the Senior Coroner, (or an appropriately experienced coroner nominated by her).

His Honour Judge Peter Thornton: I agree.

MR JUSTICE OUSELEY: In those circumstances, this application is granted, and the inquisition is quashed. There will be a new inquest in this investigation as soon as possible.

2015 INQUEST

Pre-Inquest Review Hearings (henceforth PIRHs) were convened in March, June, and in September 2015. The purpose of a PIRH is to establish the scope of the inquest, to draw up a witness list and to consider what evidence is available for the court. The remit of an inquest is narrow: Who has died? Where did they die? When did they die? How did the death come about? The first two questions were unproblematic; however, the latter questions were of vital importance in establishing a true chain of events.

Dr Wilcox, the Senior Coroner, disclosed contemporaneous police logs and other information pertaining to Carol's death. Yet Scene of Crime photographs were missing; the photographs used to identify Carol were also missing. A heated discussion took place about Dr Fisher's whereabouts. Police logs revealed that after she made the 999-emergency phone call from Manchester, Dr Fisher then made a series of telephone calls to police from her mobile phone, first from a platform at Wolverhampton railway station and later, allegedly, from Nottingham railway station. I pointed out that these journeys were not possible in the timescales stated. In any case, there is no direct train route from Wolverhampton to Nottingham. It is necessary to complete the journey by boarding a further train from Birmingham to Nottingham.

A few days before the inquest, I was warned, in a detailed and carefully worded e-mail correspondence, about contempt of court, should I go out of bounds; our relations with the coronial team deteriorated so badly that we gave serious consideration to withdrawing from the proceedings. Witness statements were served on 23 September which left insufficient time to scrutinise the evidence, and to make any necessary representations. Dr Fisher's statement was heavily redacted. Eighty-seven pages of her 106-page statement were partially, or fully redacted with whole sections blanked out. My family had waited 10 years to hear her testimony and we were appalled by this chain of events. The High Court judgement was explicit and the grounds for granting a new inquest were very clear. A dawning realisation crept up on me that the 2nd inquest would be so limited in scope that the truth about Carol's premature death would be obfuscated. Subsequently David reported the coroner to the information commissioner who referred the matter to their policy team. They ruled that we were entitled to receive Dr Fisher's statement without any redactions. The coroner responded by stating that the data protection act does not apply to coroner's courts and refused to disclose the full statement. As a result, David submitted a detailed complaint to the Ministry of Justice.

On 30 September, the coroner convened a short PIRH. I was informed that all witnesses were in attendance, and the coroner asked if my family would participate in a full inquest. I took a deep breath and observed the crowded public gallery before answering. For a moment, there was a deathly silence, and all eyes were on me.

"Yes, Ma'am."

Coroner's Officer:

"Please rise for Her Majesty's Coroner."

Coroner:

"The deceased: Carol Patricia Myers, formerly Felstead, female aged 41 years. Place of birth: Stockport. Born on 8th June 1964. Date of death: 29th of June 2005. Time of death: 16. 47. Place of death, Wandsworth. The circumstances: friend unable to make contact and requested police to make a welfare check. Police attended and got no reply at the door. Police forced entry and found her dead on the bed, wearing a T-shirt. There were tablets found in the kitchen, but no suicide note was found."

Me:

"Ma'am, may we for the record, record that the identification photographs are missing?"

Coroner:

"That will come out as part of the evidence, Mr Felstead. It's already on the record, as part of the transcript, in any case. These matters don't need to be repeated; they are already on the transcript. I turn now to a family statement to be read out at the inquest of Carol Patricia Myers nee Felstead, and this is a statement written on behalf of the family by Mr David Felstead. As part of this background, I wish to make it clear that the family absolutely protest that Carol was ever abused sexually and I'm happy that should form part of the background and that the allegations of satanic sexual abuse and murder that she made in life were investigated by the police and found to be unsubstantiated."

Our family statement was read out. The statement referred to Carol's early life and summarised her gradual estrangement from the family and the brief contact with Carol prior to her death:

"We would like to stress that Carol's medical records and psychiatric records came as a complete shock to us. We had no idea that she had been mentally and physically unwell."

The 'next of kin' – Dr Fisher

Dr Fisher gave evidence by a video link. The quality of the link was poor. On occasion, it was difficult to hear the evidence.

Coroner: (addressing the video link):

"I turn now to the first live witness, Dr Fleur Fisher. Can I be heard at the other end? Can I ask you, please, if you can swear in Dr Fisher?"

"I understand that there are some delays in the link from the Court to where you are so if you need me to pause or to ask the same question again – anything like that – please indicate that and I can slow down. I always start off well but have a terrible tendency to speed up."

A barrister represented Dr Fisher. He sat immediately to my right on the front bench before the coroner who was perched in an elevated chair directly in front of us. To his right sat counsel for the primary care trust. We were litigants in person. My family were sat in the row behind me, with friends and supporters, including a handful of colleagues from the BFMS. The remaining rows were occupied by interested observers and members of the press.

Dr Fisher was sworn in to give her live evidence.

Coroner:

"Dr Fisher, you've been invited to court today to help the Court with the sequence of events which led to and caused Carol's death and specifically because you weren't invited to give evidence at the previous inquest. I'd like to start by asking: when did you meet Carol?"

Dr Fisher:

"Well, I first met Carol on a Sunday afternoon in, I think, June 1985. I don't have the exact date because I no longer have access to the records because I am no longer in practice."

Coroner:

"In what capacity were you meeting her? As a friend or as a patient at that point? Or a doctor, I should say? I understand she then became a patient of yours for about 15 months. Is that correct?"

Dr Fisher:

"Something of that order, ma'am, yes."

Coroner:

"When did your relationship change from being doctor/patient to friend?"

Dr Fisher:

"Well, I think that was 1987, something like that."

That statement was incorrect. On 16 January 1991, Carol was placed on a three-month section in Parkside Hospital, Macclesfield, Cheshire. Dr Fisher was the hospital manager.

Coroner:

"Just so I understand, Dr Fisher, the contact with her increased and she became like a member of your extended family. Is that what you said? Yes?"

Dr Fisher:

"Yes. But during that period my own marriage broke down."

Coroner:

"Dr Fisher, that's not relevant to these proceedings."

Dr Fisher:

"No, that is right. (over-speaking)."

Coroner:

"Can we just stick, please, to the things that are matters at issue? If you can concentrate on the questions that I ask you and answer those in full."

Dr Fisher:

"Yes. (Over-speaking)."

Coroner:

"But I don't need to know any personal details about you."

Dr Fisher:

"Right. Thank you, Ma'am."

Coroner:

"How often would you say, in the last couple of years of her life, were you in contact with her?"

Dr Fisher:

"Probably, by telephone a couple of times a week."

Coroner:

"When did you last see Carol alive?"

Dr Fisher:

"I think it was probably about two weeks – 10 days to two weeks before she died."

Female Speaker:

"Excuse me."

Coroner:

"It's very difficult, isn't it, to pick up. If I can just ask you, Dr Fisher, if you can pause a moment and we will see if we can try and improve reception from your end. I am going to ask Ms I if she can turn the microphones back up. Perhaps we can just try and move it closer. Let's see if that's a little better. It isn't because now there's feedback. Ms I can you try and put it in an intermediate space? Okay. Well, let's see if we can proceed. I was just asking you when you had last seen Carol alive and you said, I believe, "It might have been about two weeks prior to her death."

Dr Fisher:

(Several inaudible words) "10 – it was either 10 days or two and a half weeks. I went up on the overnight train, went straight from the station to see Carol, spending the morning with her. I did need to go to a committee meeting after that."

Coroner:

"All right. If I can ask you to pause because I missed what you have just said and again, I remind you, Dr Fisher, I don't need to know your personal details. I just need to know evidence in relation to Carol."

Dr Fisher:

"Yes."

Coroner:

"You had come up to London and you said you went straight to Carol, and you spent the morning with her. Where was this?"

Dr Fisher testified that she visited Carol at her flat in Wandsworth.

Coroner:

"All right. How was she when you were there?"

Dr Fisher:

"She was reasonably well, I think, physically, reasonably well."

Coroner:

"I'm sorry; I can't hear you, Dr Fisher."

Dr Fisher:

"She was then in a really good situation, physically (several inaudible words). In other words, I was not particularly worried about her."

Coroner:

"How was her mood? How did it seem to you?"

Dr Fisher:

"Her mood was good."

Coroner:

"Was there any evidence to you at that time that she may want to take her own life?"

Dr Fisher:

"Absolutely not, ma'am."

Coroner:

"When did you last speak with Carol after this?"

Dr Fisher:

"I spoke with Carol on Saturday, June the 25th 2005."

Coroner:

"You raised concerns to the police on the 29th of June. Can you explain the sequence of events that led you to making this call to the police?"

Dr Fisher:

"I was worried about not hearing from Carol. On Monday, I was a bit surprised that I could not get her on the telephone."

Coroner:

"This would be Monday, 27th of June you attempted to call her and got no response?"

Dr Fisher:

"Yes."

Coroner:

"Where were you when you called 999?"

Dr Fisher:

"I was in Manchester, ma'am. I told them I was really concerned with the safety of this person and said that I thought if anything were wrong, she would likely be in her bedroom."

Coroner, referring to the computer aided dispatch (CAD):

"Looking at the entry on page one, it also says that she may have taken an overdose of drugs. Do you recall passing that information to police?"

Dr Fisher:

"I thought could it have happened?"

Coroner:

"Why did you suggest to police that she may have taken an overdose, Dr Fisher?"

Dr Fisher:

"I think it was a fear that Carol ricocheted back from her past, and I know that she had to struggle with suicidal feelings."

The coroner asked Dr Fisher about other telephone conversations which took place with police on 29 June 2005 using her mobile phone. Dr Fisher testified that she was travelling by train from Manchester, prior to getting off the train at the next station.

Coroner:

"Can you recall where you got off the train?"

Dr Fisher:

"I don't remember it, ma'am, but it's somewhere between Manchester and London."

Coroner:

"I am now going to invite Mr Kevin Felstead to ask questions on behalf of the family. I need to remind Mr Felstead we are looking at the sequence of events that led to and caused the death and the questions have to be relevant; otherwise, I have to stop you."

Me:

"I expect you to interrupt me, ma'am, if I overstep. Can I ask a question before I begin?"

Coroner:

"Yes."

Me:

"In her testimony, Dr Fisher referred to when she first met Carol. Is it agreeable that I can ask a question around that?"

Coroner:

"It depends on the question. Until I hear the question, I can't answer that. What question do you want to ask?"

Me:

"I would like to refer to part of the statement that hasn't been redacted, which says that Dr Fisher met Carol on a sunny afternoon in June 1985 and in this statement, with the bits that haven't been redacted, Carol has spoken with her about struggling because her grandmother had just died."

Coroner:

"I can't see how that is relevant. Can you explain, please?"

Me:

"Well, the relevance is this: Carol's grandmother was very much alive. So, she wasn't dead. She didn't die until 18 months later. So, what I'm trying to suggest is that the bare facts which are outlined are incorrect, multiply so. That's my point, no more."

I made an error in that statement. I have since cross-referenced this point with my grandmother's death certificate. She passed in April 1986. Nonetheless, however Carol first met Dr Fisher, it cannot have had anything to do with the bereavement of her grandmother.

Coroner:

"I'm quite happy for you to ask that question, as long as it is just limited to what you are saying."

Me:

"Yes."

Coroner:

"Thank you."

Me:

"Dr Fisher, you said that you met Carol on a sunny afternoon – I think it was a Sunday in June 1985, in your statement. You say that you spoke to Carol about the death of her grandmother. Is that correct?"

Dr Fisher:

"That is correct, Mr Felstead. But I don't have access to my clinical notes so that's the best I can do about the date. Legally, I don't have access to those notes now."

I smiled to myself at the reference "legally." As a medical ethicist, Dr Fisher knew full well that when she handed the Life Assessment to police and to the coroner's officer in 2005, that she wasn't legally entitled to access any of Carol's medical records.

Me:

"Okay. But Carol, presumably, was very upset about this event and spoke to you about it?"

Coroner:

"Mr Felstead, I think that's as far as we're going, otherwise it becomes irrelevant. I accept it to a point. Dr Fisher has answered your question and explained that's the best of her recollection."

Me:

"Am I allowed to ask a question about next of kin, ma'am?"

Coroner:

"Only next of kin in life that she was her next of kin but that is as far as it goes."

Me:

"All right. You will need to advise me here because I'm not sure what I can and can't say."

Coroner:

"Yes."

Me:

"My question would be, to Dr Fisher, is she aware that next of kin has no legal status?"

Coroner:

"That's not a relevant question."

"Okay. I'll withdraw the question," I retorted, frustratingly.

Me:

"May I ask – I can't remember, when did Dr Fisher say she last saw Carol?"

Coroner:

"She said 10 days to two weeks. She wasn't sure."

I knew Dr Fisher was on shaky ground here.

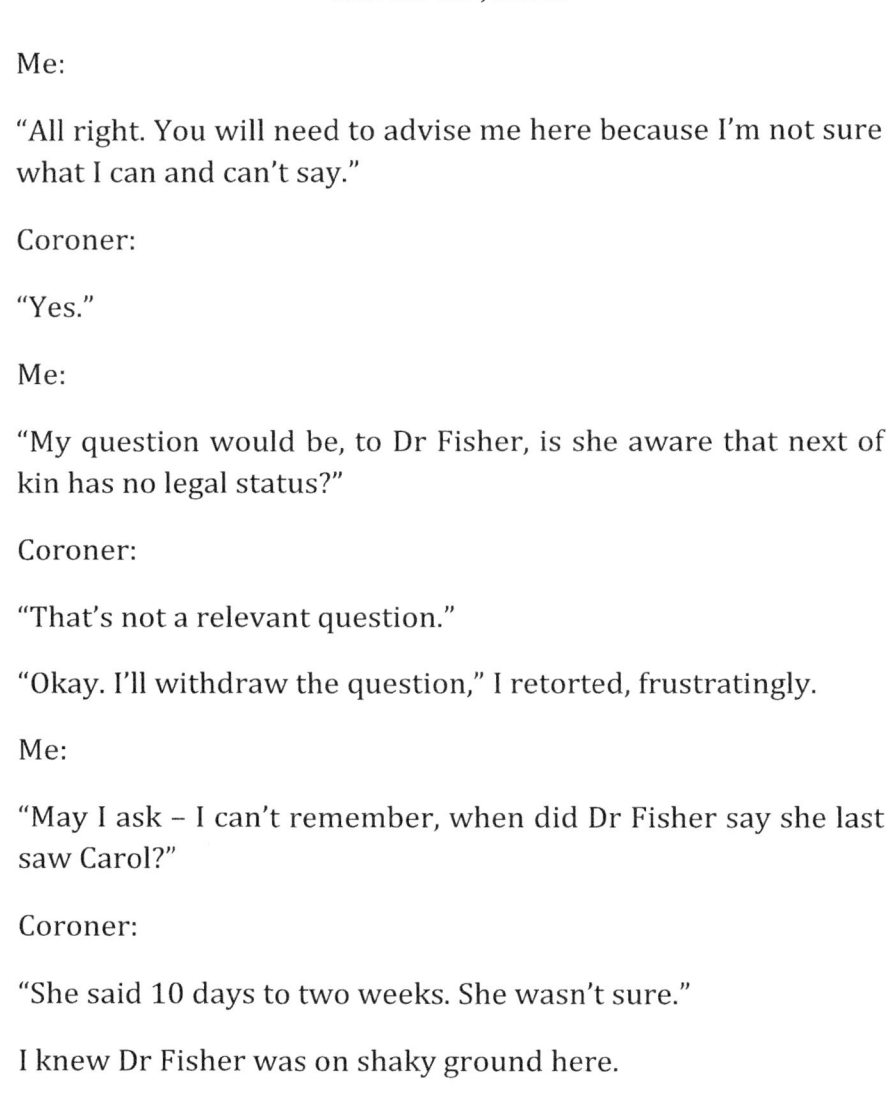

Me:

"Alright, okay. In her statement, in a conversation with Inspector T on the 29th of June, Dr Fisher told him that she saw and stayed in Carol's flat on 23rd of June. Is that correct?"

Dr Fisher:

"It may well have been; you know the dates better than I do. I don't have access to my records. There was such a catalogue of events that I think after a decade my memory is not so clear."

From my perspective, Dr Fisher's memory appeared to be very selective.

Me:

"Okay, so it might not be the 23rd. Thank you. Dr Fisher mentioned that Carol telephoned her on the Saturday, that would be the 25th. According to Carol's telephone records, of which we have copies, Carol made several telephone calls to Dr Fisher on the 25th and two telephone calls on 26th June. Is it possible you spoke to Carol on the 26th?"

Dr Fisher:

"No, it's not."

Dr Fisher:

"I don't remember; I don't remember those calls."

Coroner:

"I can't see how this is relevant. Can you explain, please?"

Me:

"All right, well that's interesting. I have the records."

Dr Fisher:

"I don't remember those calls."

Me:

"Okay, well there were two. I won't labour the point anymore but according to the telephone records, there were two telephone calls made to Dr Fisher's mobile from Carol's flat, so if it wasn't Carol perhaps someone else phoned. But I won't labour that."

Coroner:

"I haven't got the telephone records in front of me, Mr Felstead, I don't know how far this is worth going. If Dr Fisher can't remember, she can't remember. I think that's as far as we can go."

Me:

"Ok. I'm not panicking on that."

Coroner:

"Thank you anyway."

Me:

"Thank you. If we move on to events of 29 June, the journey, according to the CAD, Dr Fisher's travelling from Manchester to Plymouth. In the statement we see it's from Manchester to London and that train – it's a different train journey to get off the train and to speak to police officers. And you state that Carol will be found in the bedroom of her flat. And I've listened to what you say very carefully. Could it not be the case that if Carol had died, she could be anywhere in the flat, not just in the bedroom? She may have collapsed. Why choose in the bedroom?"

Coroner:

"I'm not sure she understood. She's answered this question before, Mr Felstead. I'll let her answer it one more time but again, it's not to repeat evidence of areas that have been in. But I'll let her answer this question but just as guidance for you because obviously you've not done this before. I'm happy to assist, alright?"

Me:

"I apologise," I said through gritted teeth.

Coroner:

"No, it's alright, Mr Felstead. I understand. That's okay. Dr Fisher, Mr Felstead just asked you that she could have been anywhere in the flat. Why did you say bedroom."

Dr Fisher testified that Carol wouldn't be cooking a "juicy stew" and that if she was feeling unwell, she believed Carol would be in her bedroom. Dr Fisher was looking tearful. I was concerned that she would turn on the waterworks. Tactically, it seemed like a good time to wrap it up. I had no further questions and the coroner released her.

The psychiatric and medical evidence.

Carol's psychiatrist was the next witness. This was the same psychiatrist who appeared at the 2005 inquest. She spoke in general terms about Carol's mental health problems and hospital admissions. She did not mention the SRA allegations, but she did state that Carol suffered from "flashbacks."

Me:

"You mentioned flashbacks; it's a term that's been used in this Court several times. What do you mean Carol suffered from flashbacks?"

Dr I:

"From my memory, it's something that she talked about, and she'd obviously had a lot of contact with the services for many years. I didn't ever discuss with her exactly the content of those or what they were. They were just something that she referred to in that way; she called them flashbacks."

Me:

"Were they flashbacks to real situations or to imagined ones?"

Dr I:

"I don't know."

The police and expert evidence

The police evidence followed. PC I repeated his testimony from the 2005 inquest. Detective I ran through the events on the day that Carol was found dead. I questioned her about the various telephone calls made by Dr Fisher on the 29th of June 2005.

Me:

"Would the CAD record mobile telephone conversations between Dr Fisher and Inspector S?"

Detective Inspector I:

"No, it wouldn't."

The time of Carol's death remained uncertain. I probed the latter point with the next witness, Dr T, an 'expert' toxicologist.

Me:

"Is there any way, from the toxicology, in estimating the date and the time of Carol's death?"

Dr T:

"Estimating time of death is very difficult. If anyone was going to do that, I would suggest that it would have been the forensic medical examiner who was called to the scene to certify death. By the time Dr X did the post-mortem examination that is far too late to make any sort of estimate. The problem is the estimation of time of death is notoriously unreliable. Pathologists tend to say, somewhat cynically perhaps, the time of death is sometime between when the person was last seen alive and when they were found dead."

Dr G, a consultant in emergency medicine, testified:

"As per my report, one thing that hasn't been mentioned is that on post-mortem examination Ms Myers was found to have a mildly dilated left ventricle which is a structural abnormality of the heart. It may be of no significance; it may be something that she's lived with that has possibly a genetic cause and has nothing to do with her cause of death. However, having a structural cardiac abnormality could make you further disposed to an arrhythmia caused by another source, for example, a toxicological source or an electrolyte imbalance which has been explained previously today."

Coroner:

"But all of this is speculation."

Dr G:

"It's all speculation."

Coroner:

"These are just possible causes, they're not probable causes?"

Dr G:

"Yes, they're possible causes."

Coroner:

"Yes. But it would be helpful to draw it together, Dr G."

Dr G:

"Okay. There is a possibility that she may have had an electrical disturbance. Low potassium could then lead to cardiac arrhythmia. Another possible cause of an electrolyte imbalance which hasn't been mentioned is in relation to another post-mortem finding which was the finding of mucus in part of the lung. That may be possible – again it's completely speculative – but it may be secondary to a chest infection."

Coroner:

"But again, these are possibilities? There's also the factor of the possible Klebsiella as well."

Dr G:

"One hypothesis is that maybe Ms Myers had developed sepsis and that had been the cause of her death. This may potentially, hypothetically, be related to an untreated Klebsiella infection. My conclusion from looking at the evidence that was in front of me was most importantly that there was not one cause that came out as a definitive cause of death."

Coroner:

"Thank you very much indeed, Dr G. Just to summarise, there are lots of different causes that could have been because we simply don't know. We don't know what the level of morphine in her blood was. It could have been drug interactions, it could have been electrolytes, it could have been a heart problem, it could have been a combination of everything, it could have been sepsis; we simply don't know."

Following a short break, the coroner rose to set out her conclusions.

Clerk of the Court:

"Please stand for Her Majesty's Coroner."

Coroner:

"Please be seated ladies and gentlemen. We've heard the evidence in this case. There will be no more, and it now falls on me to sum up my conclusions.

Before I sum up and draw my conclusions, I formally remind myself of sections 5 and 10 of the Coroners and Justice Act 2009 which states that the purpose of an investigation is to determine who the deceased was and how, when and where the deceased came by her death, and find the particulars to be registered concerning the death. The determinations may not be framed in such a way as to appear to determine any question of criminal liability on the part of a named person or civil liability.

As I consider the evidence, I am allowed to make logical inferences from evidence that I accept. The Court heard that Carol Patricia Myers, formerly known as Carol Felstead, was born in Stockport on 8th June 1964. She was found deceased at her home address on 29th of June 2005. It was a hot day, she was cool to touch, there were no signs of decomposition, and this is consistent with death of around or perhaps less than 24 hours.

The purpose of this enquiry has been to examine the sequence of events that led to and caused her death, and this has been especially pertinent for the family who had no contact with Carol since 1995. Her life was blighted by severe and enduring mental illness. There is evidence of this beginning to rear its head in the mid-1980s. Over the years she received treatment from psychiatrists, psychologists, medication. In the years in which Dr I was her responsible officer her working diagnosis was emotional unstable personality disorder.

From the evidence available to Dr I, Carol had taken overdoses on three occasions which she knew of. These overdoses were usually reported after the event such as in January 2005, some five months before her death when she had taken an overdose and then presented to the hospital afterwards. Dr I could not be sure, but she said that in her view it was usually medication that she had at home rather than medication she had gone out and purchased to take an overdose.

She was said by Dr I, whose evidence I accept, to have a higher risk of suicide of than the ordinary population. It was very difficult to be specific at any particular time. Her background risk would have been higher.

On top of this Carol suffered severe urological symptoms, and according to the evidence of Mr B and Dr I, her physical and psychological illnesses intertwined and exacerbated each other. She was diagnosed with Fowler's Syndrome, which is difficult to quantify, but the end result is urinary retention which is persistent and requires treatment. And this led on for Carol so that she had a succession of complex urological procedures.

Dr Fisher said she was in regular contact with Carol. When she was no longer in London she would come up and call in and visit her. According to Dr Fisher when she gave evidence live, and I note that this is some 10 years after the event, she felt that she had last seen Carol 10 days or two weeks or so before her death when she had called in and visited her in her flat. There is evidence provided through the Incident Management Log with which I was assisted by Detective Inspector I, that at the time Dr Fisher, when she had been speaking to police and such matters were recorded, was noted to have last seen Carol on 23rd June 2005, and had last spoken to her on 27th June 2005. When this was put to her in questions by Mr Kevin Felstead, who has done an incredible job today, Dr Fisher said she couldn't really remember, and I make a finding of fact based upon evidence that was recorded at the time in the Incident Management Log that she did in fact see her on 23rd June, and last spoke to her on 27th June, and that would be in keeping with the questions from Mr Felstead in which he referred to phone records.

Toxicology revealed the presence of various prescribed medications, a low level of alcohol that either could have been imbibed by Carol or be the result of post-bacterial production.

I note that post-mortem there were no signs of injury to Carol's body. It was just some lividity which was settling in the blood on the arms, and Mr T's evidence was that this can happen within hours of death.

Drugs within her bloodstream were all at therapeutic levels other than two drugs, mirtazapine and even promethazine which were at the highest therapeutic level but well below any toxic levels.

I am satisfied that that there is no evidence of any accidental injury that has caused or contributed to Carol's death. That can be excluded. I cannot exclude whether Carol took an overdose of morphine, and I also have a wide range of natural cause events which together or separately could have led to and caused Carol's death. In these circumstances there is simply no sufficient evidence of a cause of Carol's death that would allow me to record any short form verdict or conclusion as I should now more properly say. All speculation and no probabilities in these circumstances. I have no option but to record an open conclusion.

When I consider the evidence in the round, and attempt from this evidence to draw conclusions in which I can be satisfied to the required legal standard, I am entirely satisfied that there is nothing suspicious in Carol's death, that there is no evidence of third-party involvement. The evidence of Mr T that she had been dead around 24 hours, that she was found within a locked and secure accommodation and that there were no signs of disturbance or disruption; all of these things mitigate entirely against anything suspicious.

That concludes this inquiry. All that remains is for me to thank first of the family for the assistance they have given to this inquiry with pieces of evidence that they had for the past Court and providing investigative lines for this court to file.

I would like to thank witnesses without whose help I would not have been able to reach any conclusions at all.

Most importantly, I would like to pass my sympathy to Carol's family. What you have been through since you had that call from my Coroner's Officer, Sharon Marshall, all those years ago is unimaginable. The Court regrets that I cannot give you any firm conclusions today, but I hope that you will be able to accept that I have investigated the death as far as I am able to, and I really wish you all very well.

I particularly would like to thank Mr Felstead. For someone who has never assisted a Court before, you did a fabulous job."

Me:

"Thank you very much, madam."

Coroner:

"Thank you."

Clerk of the Court:

"Court rise."

Coroner:

"Good afternoon, ladies and gentlemen."

Epilogue

The Open Verdict was not unexpected. While the court was in recess, I sat in the public area with a journalist from the *Times* newspaper. He had pre-empted the verdict and later wrote a piece about the inquest. Prior to the inquest, our case was widely reported in the national press. 'High Court to Grant Landmark Inquest into Nurse Death Mystery' typified the headlines. The inquest also received extensive coverage in the national, and international, press. The Irish Examiner, the Irish Independent, and the Evening Standard were the first to report on the case. The following day, many more newspapers followed suit, including the Daily Telegraph, with a headline, 'Satanic Sex Abuse Claims Were a Myth,' Nurse's Family Tells Inquest. The Evening Standard reported:

A nurse died after claiming she had been sexually abused by a Satanic cult, an inquest heard. But a police investigation found that the disturbing allegations were unsubstantiated, and her family believe they were false memories dreamt up during controversial recovered memory sessions. The brother of Miss Myers, who was born Carol Felstead but changed her name, said the claims were a "myth."

Kevin Felstead told Westminster Coroner's Court, which was sitting at the Royal Courts of Justice, that her family "fiercely contest the allegations." Addressing the court, Mr Felstead said: "I just want to ask that the court acknowledges that Carol developed false memories that were demonstrably not true."

Coroner Fiona Wilcox said: "she could not rule that Ms Myers suffered from false memories. But she acknowledged the extreme allegations that were made of Satanic sexual abuse and murder were investigated and found to be unsubstantiated." She added: "I wish to be clear that the family absolutely protest that Carol was abused sexually, and the allegations of Satanic sexual abuse and murder that she made in life were investigated by police and found to be unsubstantiated."

The police investigation was initiated by us against Dr Fisher. The whereabouts of Dr Fisher when, in 2005, she made the 999-emergency phone call to the Metropolitan Police Service (MPS) was puzzling. This matter was not resolved to our satisfaction in the PIRHs nor during the full 2015 inquest hearing. I requested written and audio transcripts of the hearings, which arrived in due course. We then poured over the evidence, scrutinising the transcripts in minute detail. One fact stood out. If Dr Fisher was in Manchester when she telephoned police raising concerns that Carol may have taken her own life, why was she connected to the call centre for the MPS? We checked the policies and procedures of British Telecom, together with the two police forces. Accordingly, Dr Fisher's call would have been put through to the call centre for Greater Manchester Police (GMP)

since it would not be possible to make a telephone call in the Manchester area and to then be connected to London police. This principle applies nationwide, and for good reason. When an individual telephones 999, the call is received by a BT operator who will ask the caller which emergency service they require. If the service required is the police, the BT operator will transfer the call to the force control room in the local area. The BT operator will then pass the telephone call to the call-taker. This process cannot be avoided. If Dr Fisher was in Manchester as she claimed in her witness statement and in her live testimony in the coroner's court, she would have automatically been transferred to GMP because she was physically in the Manchester area. Dr Fisher rang 999 and was connected to the MPS, therefore she must have been physically present in the London area at the time she was making the telephone call. It is not possible to telephone 999 in Manchester and to then be connected directly to the MPS.

How emergency 999 calls are received by the police

The correct sequence of events would be as follows: Dr Fisher would telephone 999. A BT operator would ask her which emergency service she required, Police, Fire, or Ambulance. Dr Fisher would state that she required the police. Dr Fisher would then be connected to greater manchester police (GMP) who would record details of the incident, including her telephone number. GMP would immediately forward details of the incident together with Dr Fisher's contact details. They would contact the MPS in one of two ways two ways (1); GMP would telephone the MPS; (2) they would send the relevant details electronically. Once the MPS were in receipt of the information, and given that it is an emergency, a matter of life and death no less, they would then deploy the appropriate resources. They may then telephone Dr Fisher for further information.

Following a Freedom of Information Request to GMP to clarify this process, their Information Compliance & Records Unit responded as follows:

"The Greater Manchester Police would record the details then contact the Metropolitan Police with the details and back this up with a fax. Greater Manchester Police would not grade this call, this would be done by the Metropolitan Police based on the information provided by Greater Manchester Police.

Both forces would make a computerised log of the incident including the actions taken; the Greater Manchester Police one would close quickly once the details are passed to the other force."

From the Inquest Transcript 30 September 2015:

Coroner, addressing a police inspector:

"I want you to talk first through the CAD Printout that has been supplied. Can you assist me with this because I have been struggling to understand it? I understand this to be a printout of the calls as they come in, and the actions as they come in. Is that correct?"

Detective Inspector I:

"Okay. So, when a call goes into the police, so using the 999 system, a CAD is generated. So, it's on a computer and it's – there's somebody there, an operator, who types in what the caller is saying, and makes notes so that officers can be deployed to the scene of an incident and the appropriate people attend. This is kept on a system, so you can look back at it, and it's called a CAD, and each CAD is given a number and it's dated, timed, with the details of every call that comes in."

Coroner:

"So, if I have understood you, it's a contemporaneous record by typists typing as the call is made?"

Detective Inspector I:

"That is correct."

Coroner:

"Is that correct?"

Detective Inspector I:

"That is correct."

Coroner:

"So, if I take you first to what I understand to be the first call, on page one of this in relation to this death if we look at the date at the top. It is entered at 15: 14, 29th June 2005 and we can see: Caller is a friend of Carol Myers. Serious concerns female may have taken an overdose of drugs. She has contacted St Georges Hospital. She cannot get hold of her on her mobile. Caller states female will be in her bedroom, which is in the rear of the property. I understand this is what the typist then will have recorded when Dr Fisher called. Is that correct?"

Detective Inspector I:

"Yes."

The Coroner and DI are confirming that the 999 call was in fact not received by GMP, but by the Met Police, meaning that Dr Fisher made that telephone call from the London catchment area.

In her 2015 statement to police Dr Fisher states:

"So, I rang 999 from Manchester and I got on the train to go down to London. It hadn't been my plan originally. I went down to London."

From our perspective, we had participated in three PIRHs and two full inquests and Dr Fisher's whereabouts on the day that Carol was pronounced dead remained unclear. After careful consideration of the evidence, and much discussion amongst ourselves, David Felstead prepared a meticulous application to overturn the second inquest. We found ourselves in new territory: could the Solicitor General be persuaded for a second time about the merits of our argument? We sifted through the evidence, paying careful attention to every detail. This process took several months. Our first complaint point was on the ground that, when Dr Fisher testified at the 2nd inquest, under oath, she was in Manchester when she made the 999-emergency phone call. Therefore, Dr Fisher committed perjury because she must in fact have made that call from a geographical location within the catchment of the metropolitan police service; otherwise, Dr Fisher could not have been connected to a call centre for the metropolitan police.

On10 January 2017, a 64-page application was submitted to the Attorney General's Office. It was detailed and evidence-based. We created an index of supporting documents including the full inquest transcripts and transcripts of the PIRHs, together with the 2014 rare legal authorisation (*fiat*) from the Solicitor General. In total it amounted to several hundred pages which were then paginated and appended to the application. My father and I took the train to London, paid the application fee, and filed the claim in person, in the claim's office based within the Royal

Courts of Justice. When we finally handed it in, we were satisfied with our efforts and confident about the logic of our argument.

Our main complaint points were focused on what we contended were irregularity of proceedings and insufficiency of enquiry.

The legal threshold to be granted permission from the Solicitor General to apply to the High Court is understandably very high. Nonetheless the application was successful. From the Attorney General's website:

Family of Carol Myers can apply for fresh inquest.

Solicitor General gives consent for the family of Carol Myers to apply to the High Court for a fresh inquest into her death.

18 October 2017

The Solicitor General Robert Buckland QC MP has today given consent for the family of Carol Patricia Myers to apply to the High Court for a fresh inquest into the circumstances surrounding her death.

Carol Myers, 41, was found dead by the Metropolitan Police Service on 29th June 2005. The first inquest took place on 4 July 2005 and the coroner recorded an open verdict. A second inquest took place on 30 September 2015 and an open verdict was given again.

The Solicitor General stated:

"Having considered the application, I have given consent to the family of Carole Myers to apply to the High Court for a new inquest into her death. I am satisfied that it is in the interests of justice for the application for a new inquest to be heard by the High Court."

The Solicitor General has the authority to decide whether an application can be made to the High Court for a new inquest to be opened. He has no power to order a new coronial inquest himself. A new inquest can only be ordered by the High Court on an application made either by the Attorney or by a third party with the consent of the Attorney.

Before an application can be made, the Attorney or Solicitor has to be satisfied that there is a reasonable prospect that the Court will be persuaded to open a new inquest. These decisions are made as part of his public interest function, independently of Government and strictly on the basis of the evidence. The Solicitor concluded, in this case, that there were sufficient grounds of challenge set out in the application to have a reasonable chance of success.

David submitted a detailed application to the High Court. On 21 November and we were entered on the Warned List. The coroner failed to respond to the application within the designated timescales and we argued that she was now out of time and therefore should be struck out of the proceedings. On 7 December the coroner was granted an extension by Master Gidden in the Queen's Bench Division Administrative Court to file and serve written evidence by 4.00 pm on 17 January, on the following grounds:

The Claimant seeks an order to quash a second inquest into the death of his sister, Carol Myers, who died in June 2005. The Claimant's opposition to the application is entirely understandable but in the overall circumstances in which the parties now find themselves it is unlikely to be to any advantage to the Defendant to be compelled to respond to the claim without the extension of time that the application explains is necessary. In my view sufficient reason has been given and the additional two months is not unreasonable given the lengthy passage of time since 2005, the long history of proceedings and events that have followed and the extraordinary prospect of what would be a third inquest.

On 18 December the coroner submitted to the High Court her First Witness Statement. She addressed the SRA allegations noting that:

The Felstead family obtained more information about the supposed allegations and took the view that they were the result of false memories developed in therapy sessions.

To our surprise, the coroner insisted that Dr Fisher's location when she made the emergency 999 telephone call to police was of "marginal relevance to the facts which the inquest had to determine." Clearly, the Solicitor General took the opposite view, otherwise our application would have been rejected.

We reflected carefully about our next move and the coroner's stance in opposing the application. It is important to note that the coroner is supported by an active litigation team funded by the taxpayer. We were Litigants in Person responsible for our own legal costs. While we were unfazed by the prospect of fresh legal proceedings, we were concerned about potential costs – which can be incurred even if the application is successful. As the applicant, David Felstead was particularly concerned about costs in the likely event that proceedings became protracted. The only comparable case, which we had been observing from a distance, was Carmel Bloom who died in Essex in September 2002, aged 54. Bloom underwent a kidney stone operation and died from complications following surgery and "a lack of monitoring and communication." There were three inquests into her death. The third inquest was ordered in 2014 and was convened in the RCJ in October 2016. Bernard Bloom, the brother of the deceased, spent over three million pounds in legal fees. He described the 3rd inquest as a "whitewash" and a "stitch up." David had been monitoring this case closely, and he was aware that if costs were awarded against him, whatever the outcome, he could lose his home and be subjected to bankruptcy proceedings. With considerable reluctance, he withdrew from the proceedings. In retrospect, this was to become a watershed moment for completely different reasons.

Exhumation

Christmas came and passed. David, not one to give up easily, telephoned one evening: "I think that we should apply to the Ministry of Justice for an exhumation licence." An additional complaint point in our application to the attorney general's office concerned the identification process supposedly used to identify Carol. We were sceptical in the extreme about the official narrative that the Coroner's Officer took a photograph of Carol in the morgue and later compared it with a photograph supplied by Dr Fisher, using a "Polaroid camera." Both photographs were missing, as were some scene of crime photographs. This matter was the focus of intense debate in the 2015 PIRHs. We initially viewed scene of crime photographs in a police station in 2009. They were also missing, although later, after we supplied reference numbers, some of the photographs were traced.

The coroner's file contained a death cover sheet which recorded Carol's name together with a unique reference number. However, the file also housed a separate death sheet which recorded the name of a different deceased person (female) with the same reference number. The 2nd Inquest did not allay our concerns about these matters. Back in 2006, we considered applying for an exhumation licence, but we were advised by a

Home Office Pathologist that it might be more prudent to instigate proceedings to quash the 2005 inquest.

On 12 April 2018 we applied to the Ministry of Justice for a licence to exhume Carol's body. On 25 April, the licence was granted. On 5 June, in what I would describe as an extremely traumatic day for the family, the exhumation was carried out. Carol's body was transported to a local hospital for pathological analysis supervised by a Senior Home Office Pathologist. When the pathology was completed, her body was re-reburied.

The following day, we provided DNA samples for comparative purposes. On 22 June we received official confirmation from a Forensic Laboratory which established definitively that the deceased was in fact Carol. The DNA results are conclusive, and we have no doubts at all that Carol has been positively identified. It was an immense relieve and the result we had hoped for. As it is now 19 years since Carol died, it is impossible to do further toxicological analysis to establish a definitive cause of death. Therefore, it remains highly unlikely that we will ever find an actual cause of death. We now accept that the exhumation is the nearest we will get to closure with regards to Carol's death.

PART 3
THE BFMS 2014 – 2023

The BFMS published *Fractured Families* in 2007 and *Miscarriages of Memory* in 2010. These seminal publications highlighted the real-life dangers of false memory-type allegations. The forward to *Miscarriages of Memory* was written by the Right Honourable Earle Howe, Parliamentary Under Secretary of State, Department of Health, and formerly Vice-Chair of the All-Party Parliamentary Group for Abuse Allegations.

The phenomenon of false memory first came to my attention some years ago when I received a letter from a mother who asked me to meet her, and the story she told me was truly appalling. She and her husband were professional people with three grown-up children. The youngest was a 17-year-old daughter who had received counselling for depression and then, suddenly, stopped talking to her parents. When she did start talking to them, the things she said totally shattered the family. She maintained she had been able to remember, in considerable detail, being repeatedly sexually abused by her father from about the age of four, these memories having been locked away and completely forgotten until she entered counselling. The father was adamant that never in his life would he have done the things he was being accused of. Later, when the specific dates and times were looked at, it was quite clear that it would have been impossible for many to have taken place. Thus, it was that having been alerted to the question of whether therapies may exert a harmful power on the mind, particularly of those who are already vulnerable, I raised the matter in the House of Lords (Lords Hansard 17 October 2001, column 645).

This book traces the effects which the theory of recovered memory has had on our legal processes, civil and criminal; and the sway it has held over professional bodies and looks at its spread across the globe. It evokes a glimmer, perhaps no more, of the damage done to loving and united families.

Five years ago, as Opposition Health spokesman in the House of Lords and Deputy Chairman of the all-party committee on abuse investigations, I was invited to address the Annual General Meeting of the British False Memory Society. I was happy to see this as an opportunity to call for more openness and scepticism in the legal system and social services when dealing with abuse allegations.

It was the issue of memories of childhood abuse, allegedly recovered by adults who had no prior knowledge of the abuse until undergoing therapy – that decided me to accept the invitation.

My audience of 100, mostly parents and grandparents, had one thing in common: they had all been accused of child abuse. Some had been arrested, others were acquitted in court, a few were found guilty and imprisoned.

Others had been released on appeal or had served their sentence and were seeking to prove their innocence. Some of their stories are told here.

As for the family whose story began this foreword, the young woman continued to elaborate her account and claimed to have 'remembered' –

again while undergoing therapy – being sexually assaulted by her brother. This was alleged to have happened at a time when she shared a room with her sister who asserted vehemently that nothing wrong had ever taken place.

This story echoes similar ones that I have since received from other families. Where such statements cannot be easily disproved, as in the above case, the police and social services are drawn in. The accused – usually, but not always, a father – may find himself involved in a desperate attempt to disprove allegations reaching back 20 or 30 years.

Childhood medical and school records may have been destroyed and there may be little more evidence to use in defence other than character references and the accused's word that nothing of the sort happened.

It is these cases – 672 known to the BFMS where legal enquiries followed – that underline the need for this book, *Miscarriage of Memory*. In describing in my Lords speech how false allegations can arise, I said:

"If there was one overriding observation, I could make about any of the phenomena associated with wrongful allegations it is the extraordinary absence of scepticism which has allowed those phenomena to flourish and gain public acceptance."

I congratulate the Society on having produced this book, *Miscarriage of Memory*, and commend it as standard reading for all who are interested in maintaining the highest levels of justice within the legal system.

The creation of a serial killer – Thomas Quick

An extreme example of how the criminal justice system can malfunction when allegations are based on false memories is illustrated by the extraordinary case of Thomas Quick (real name Sture Bergwall). Quick was Sweden's most notorious serial killer. He confessed to 39 murders and was convicted and sentenced to life imprisonment for eight murders. In his book, *The Strange Case of Thomas Quick: the Swedish Serial Killer and the Psychoanalyst Who Created Him* (Portobello Books, 2015), Dan Josephsson describes how, during the summer of 1992, Quick together with his psychotherapist, psychiatric nurses, a memory expert, the police, and his solicitor were searching in the Orji Forest for the bones of one of his murder victims. Thomas Quick was not in fact a serial killer, but he is Sweden's most notorious miscarriage of justice. In 2013, the Swedish government instigated a public inquiry which resulted in major reform to their criminal justice system.

The blurb to journalist Josephsson's book, provides a useful summary of Quick's fantastical allegations:

In 1991 Sture Bergwall, a petty criminal and drug addict, botched an armed robbery so badly that he was deemed to be more in need of therapy than punishment. He was committed to Sater, Sweden's equivalent of Broadmoor, and began a course of psychotherapy and psychoactive drugs. During the therapy, he began to recover memories so vicious and traumatic that he had repressed them: sickening scenes of childhood abuse, incest, and torture, which led to a series of brutal murders in his adult years. He eventually confessed to raping, killing, and even eating more than thirty victims. Embracing the process of self-discovery, he took on a new name: Thomas Quick. He was brought to trial and convicted of eight murders.

In 2008, his confessions were proved to be entirely fabricated and every single conviction was overturned. In this gripping book, Dan Josefsson uncovers the tangled web of deceptions and delusions that emerged within the Quick team. He reveals how a sick prisoner and mental patient, addled with prescription drugs and desperate for validation, allowed himself to become a case study for a sect-like group of therapists who practised the controversial method of 'recovered memory therapy.' The group's leader, psychoanalyst Margit Norwell, hoped that her study of Thomas Quick would make history.

This is a riveting story about how pseudoscientific therapy and the irrational belief system of a secretive group of otherwise intelligent people caused the most spectacular miscarriage of justice in modern Swedish history. It is told by one of Sweden's foremost investigative journalists.

In a revealing interview with journalist, Elizabeth Day (the *Guardian* newspaper 20 October 2012), Quick revealed how his false memories were created:

I'd go to the Royal Library in Stockholm on day release and read upon old cases on the newspaper microfiches. A lot happened inside of me. I'd get high, I'd get a kick and then I'd have lots of fantasies. My imagination would run wild. In one sense, they gave me a lot of creativity. It was like a vicious circle. The more I told, the more attention I got from the therapists and the police and the memory experts, and that meant I also got more drugs.

Which just about sums up this sorry saga.

The Hampstead SRA Hoax

In P and Q (Children: Care Proceedings: Fact finding), Justice Pauffley delivered a detailed judgement about an extraordinary Satanic panic in London. Extracts of which are quoted below.

From the Judgement:

In September 2014, lurid allegations of the most serious kind were drawn to the attention of the Metropolitan Police. In a variety of ways, it was suggested that P and Q were part of a large group of children from North London who had been sexually abused, made to abuse one another and that they had belonged to a satanic cult in which there was significant paedophile activity.

Specifically, it was said that babies were supplied from all over the world. They were bought, injected with drugs, and then sent by TNT or DHL to London. The assertions were that babies had been abused, tortured, and then sacrificed. Their throats were slit, blood was drunk, and cult members would then dance wearing babies' skulls (sometimes with blood and hair still attached) on their bodies. All the cult members wore shoes made of baby skin produced by the owner of a specified shoe shop.

Children, it was alleged, would be anally abused by adult members of the cult using plastic penises or "willies."

Christchurch primary school in Hampstead was said to be where the "main action" occurred but at least seven other schools were named. East Finchley swimming pool was identified as one of the other meeting venues for the paedophile ring. Rituals were performed, so it was claimed, in an upstairs room at the McDonald's restaurant where the "boss" allowed child sacrifice because he was a member of the cult. Human babies were prepared, cooked in the ovens within a secret kitchen and then eaten by cult members.

Justice Pauffley was unequivocal in her assessment:

I am able to state with complete conviction that none of the allegations are true. The claims are baseless. Those who have sought to perpetuate them are either evil and/or foolish. All the indications are that over a period of some weeks last summer, P and Q were forced to provide accounts of horrific events. The stories came about as the result of relentless emotional and psychological pressure as well as significant physical abuse. Torture is a strong word, but it is the most accurate to describe what has been done to the children by Mr Christie and Ms Draper (mother and partner). The children were assaulted by Mr Christie by being hit with a metal spoon on multiple occasions over their head and legs, by being pushed into walls, punched, and kicked. Water was poured over them as they knelt semi-clothed.

As investigative journalist and author Rosie Waterhouse asserted, "the vast majority of academic researchers have long since concluded that Satanic ritual abuse is a myth." Yet belief in SRA continues in the 21st century. Dr Waterhouse reported on a disturbing case (the *Sunday Times*, 3 October 2021) which was heard in Caernarfon Crown Court in North Wales culminating in the conviction and imprisonment of a Christian councillor and her conspirators for child kidnap. This case is extreme by any comparison, but it illustrates that the myth of SRA continues to endure in the 21st century. (Editor's note: Dr Waterhouse was awarded a doctorate from City University (London) in 2014 – entitled: *Satanic abuse, false memories, and moral panics: Anatomy of a 24-year investigation*. A leading authority on the subject, she has been investigating SRA allegations for over three decades).

The trial resulted in the conviction of six individuals for conspiracy to kidnap a child, at knifepoint, and in broad daylight; the perpetrators believed they were saving the boy from the clutches of a Satanic Cult based on the Isle of Anglesey. The boy's father (who cannot be named for legal reasons) was supposed to be a member of the Cult. Judge Nicola Jones presided over the trial. Janet Stevenson, a Christian counsellor who claimed to specialise in treating alleged victims of SRA, Anke Hill, a client, and William Wong, a long-standing believer in the myth of SRA, snatched the child after school had ended; Wong threatened the child's foster mother at knifepoint. They were later apprehended by police armed response officers in Northamptonshire.

Hill and Stevenson intended to drive the boy from North Wales to Stevenson's home in Crawley, Sussex, after driving to and from Wales on the M1 motorway. They planned to later take the child to Europe. During cross-examination Stevenson claimed, bizarrely, that her actions did not constitute a criminal offence because she was trying to safeguard the child:

> People during the Second World War, who were trying to smuggle children out of concentration camps in suitcases or bags put themselves at risk that they would be shot by the Gestapo. It was an offence, but it was morally right because they were saving children. I could not bear anybody's child being sexually abused, manipulated, tortured, and potentially murdered.

During evidence, the court heard how Stevenson and her husband, Edward, rented a hire car to take the child out of Wales. Two other members of the group acted as lookouts from bridges in North Wales. In a press release on 30 September 2021, the Crown Prosecution Service stated: "the facts of the case are chilling, and it must have been a terrifying experience for the child and carer." Judge Jones imposed lengthy custodial sentences on the accused. Janet Stevenson was sentenced to 15 years and five years on extended licence; William Wong was sentenced to 17 years plus a further five years on extended licence; Anke Hill was sentenced to 14 years and five months and five years on extended licence. All six defendants were given indefinite restraining orders.

Sentencing Wong, Judge Jones remarked, "You purport to be an expert on satanic ritual abuse. You have interviewed vulnerable victims of abuse yet have no training or qualifications in this respect." She ruled further that Hill's views about SRA were entrenched.

RENEWED MEDIA INTEREST

As we moved into 2013, Madeline Greenhalgh had been working at the coalface for the previous 20 years and decided to take more of a backseat ensuring that the Society remained compliant with the various procedures set out by the Charity Commission. To reduce overheads, the BFMS restructured closing its full-time office in Bath in favour of home working. I came into post as Director of Communications in 2014. My main role was to further raise awareness of the BFMS.

Consequently, the BFMS began to receive a considerable number of media enquiries. In 2017, for example, the July/August edition of *Wired* magazine published a detailed article on false memory, entitled 'The Memory Hacker.' The piece featured a profile of Dr Julia Shaw (then a member of our Scientific and Professional Advisory Board). I attended a photoshoot with Julia at Southbank University and participated in telephone interviews before the magazine went to publication. The article contained a few short case histories – both old and new – including a section about former Prime Minister Sir Edward Heath who was deceased but nonetheless the subject of a police operation launched in 2015 by Wiltshire police. The Edward Heath allegations received widespread media coverage. One of Heath's multiple accusers, known as Lucy X, had received hypnotherapy prior to making allegations. The extraordinary allegations made against Heath included SRA and murder. The police operation which was later shut down is estimated to have cost over £1 million pounds. The *Wired* article concluded with a quotation from Distinguished Professor of Psychology Elizabeth Loftus who has suggested that criminal courts consider adopting a new oath: "Do you swear to tell the truth, the whole truth, or whatever it is you think you remember?"

A couple of months later, I was reading press coverage about an unusual trial at Blackfriars' Crown Court involving regression therapy. After the jury returned Not Guilty verdicts, the *Times* journalist David Brown published on 21 September a particularly good article covering the case. I was later contacted by his colleague, Georgie Keates, who interviewed me about the caseload of the BFMS.

Later that day, Keates posted two short articles on the home page of the *Times online* newspaper, including a short piece about Carol Felstead. The articles were amalgamated and published in the printed edition of the *Times* the following day, under the title of 'Nonsense therapy investigated after abuse allegations.' Other newspapers adopted a similar perspective, and on 24 September, Sarah Baxter, writing in the *Sunday Times*, reported on the Blackfriars trial with a very good piece entitled 'Quack therapy drives a troubled family to tragedy.'

Georgie Keates' article grabbed the attention of *BBC London News* who wanted to speak to me about false memory in general and about the Carol Felstead case specifically. On 29 September 2017 I boarded a train to London with my father. We were interviewed and filmed in a local pub and the broadcast went out at prime time following the national news. Julia Shaw was interviewed in the BBC studio. The main thrust of the programme was that psychotherapy ought to be more robustly regulated:

Campaigners are calling for better regulation of the psychotherapy industry and are warning that some psychotherapists are implanting false memories into the minds of vulnerable people. The family of one London nurse are raising awareness of the issue after she falsely accused them of murder.

The BBC additionally put a link to the broadcast on Facebook; a short video clip of the interview was also released.

A few days later, I undertook a series of telephone interviews with Antonia Hoyle (*Daily Mail*) who dispatched a photographer to my house. On 11 October, 'What made them falsely accuse their dads of sex abuse?' appeared in the 'Femail' section of the *Mail*. The article discussed three BFMS case studies – Alan White, Maxine Berry, and Carol Felstead. Professor Chris French gave an interview. Discussing recovered memory therapists, he asserted:

Sadly, some psychotherapists are still using these dangerous techniques. Society finds it easy to accept the idea that a victim of abuse has repressed the memory and that a skilled therapist can bring it to the surface. But there is little evidence to support the idea that a traumatic experience will be pushed into the unconscious mind. You are far more likely to remember a traumatic event than to forget it.

In October 2017, BBC Radio 3 broadcast a series of programmes on the nature of memory under the generic heading, 'The Strangeness of Memory,' which included interviews with BFMS advisory board members. Professor Chris French's talk was entitled, 'False Memories: Examining childhood memories and analysing their accuracy;' Professor Fiona Gabbert's talk was entitled, 'The Fallibility of Memory.'

A few days later, as discussed in chapter 6, on 17 October, the Solicitor General gave authorisation for the family of Carol Felstead to apply to the High Court to seek permission to quash the second inquest into her death. This was an extraordinary development, and the press were quick to notice it. The first journalist to cover the story was David Brown. I undertook a telephone interview with the *Times* within an hour of the ruling. The article was published the following day – 'Family of satanic sex abuse nurse can seek third inquest.' The piece went further than anything previously published on the topic. Later that evening, I was sitting in a local tapas restaurant when my mobile phone rang. "Hello, my name is Gareth Davies. I'm calling from the *Mail online*. Are you available to undertake a telephone interview?" A few hours later the *Mail* published (with slight embellishment) a particularly good piece entitled: 'Family of a nurse who died in Mysterious circumstances after falsely claiming that her father ran a Satanic cult and impregnated her are awarded a third inquest to determine what caused her death.' The following day, I participated in a telephone interview with Alison Maloney from the *Sun online*. I was uncertain about what stance the *Sun* would adopt and I was pleasantly surprised with what turned out to be another very excellent article replete with eight photographs.

CREATING HYSTERIA: CARL BEECH

I attended parts of the Carl Beech trial in July 2019. The scene outside Newcastle Crown Court was awash with satellite vehicles representing the mainstream media. In court, most of the national press and television broadcasters had dispatched journalists to cover the trial. The atmosphere was electric. The *Times* newspaper covered the case daily in separate articles, normally released at 1.00 pm followed by an early evening press release. One day, the man who I had been reading about since he first reported allegations to police, after Tom Watson MP rose to his feet during Prime Minister's Questions in October 2012, to announce that he had evidence about an establishment paedophile ring based in Westminster, was sat in the glass dock immediately behind me.

This sorry saga has exposed the shambolic investigations of historic abuse claims in the UK. Beech was convicted of 12 counts of perverting the course of justice and of fraudulently claiming compensation from the Criminal Injuries Compensation Authority. Beech, aka 'Nick' accused several prominent figures including former Home Secretary Leon Brittan (who died with allegations hanging over him); Lord

Bramall (a former head of the army); Lord Janner (a former Labour MP); Harvey Proctor (a former Conservative MP); and former Prime Minister, Sir Edward Heath (deceased, 2005). Beech also accused, Sir Morris Oldfield, a former head of M16; Sir Michael Hanley, previously Director of M15 and Field Marshall Sir Roland Gibbs.

Beech accused the men of being part of an organised paedophile network responsible for rape, torture, and murder. "I was physically, emotionally and sexually abused by my stepfather and a paedophile ring of 20 men," alleged Beech who had pleaded guilty to possessing indecent images. During the trial it emerged that Beech previously delivered child abuse training to primary school children on behalf of the NSPCC. Carl Beech began his career working as a paediatric nurse; he was subsequently employed as a manager for the Healthcare Quality Commission.

In his opening speech, Tony Baddenoch QC for the prosecution, said: "This case concerns the making of false allegations of the most serious kind." The false allegations included three child murders, multiple rapes, kidnapping and widespread sexual abuse against young boys. "It is quite impossible to conceive of allegations of a worse kind to be made." Beech claimed that he had suffered physical and sexual abuse, including rape. He accused former heads of M15 and M16 whom he claimed, "were responsible for abuse and forms of torture" in the form of "electric shocks and having darts thrown at him." Beech alleged that he had been "taken to parties" where he was abused in a variety of locations. These included: Dolphin Square, military barracks, the Elm Guest House, the Carlton Club, Heathrow Airport, London Zoo, Brighton, Sir Edward Heath's house and on the yacht of the former Prime Minister. In 2014, police said in a press conference that the allegations were "credible and true."

Baddenoch, addressing the court, said that the allegations were "a complete fabrication." They are "incredible and untrue."

Beech claimed to have witnessed the murder of Martin Allen who disappeared in London in 1979, aged 15. Kevin Allen, the brother of Martin, was contacted in 2014 by the Metropolitan Police Service. He was informed that police had received information alleging his brother had been abducted by a paedophile murder ring. "The source of that false hope to Kevin," the prosecution stated, "35 years after his brother went missing, was ultimately the false allegations of this defendant, Carl Beech."

His anonymity was removed after a judge ruled that it was in the interests of justice for Beech to be named. The Met Police closed the investigation in 2016 and no arrests were made. The case was later referred to Northumbria Police. They "found that key elements" of the story were totally unfounded and the untrue allegations began to unfold. Beech's home was raided, and electronic devises were seized. His lurid fantasies were remarkable. Beech claimed that "a boy had been murdered by Harvey Proctor, raped and stabbed." Beech told police that he held his hand and was told "that he was next. Another boy was murdered after the abusers asked the boys to elect who should be murdered."

Beech, aged 46, alleged that the abuse started when he was aged seven, and stopped before he was 16. He was subsequently allocated a police liaison officer "to assist him and to support him in the process." In interview with Northumbria Police, Beech declined to comment and he "fled the country and lived oversees as a fugitive." A special fugitive agency in Sweden secured his arrest, working with the National Crime Agency utilising a European Arrest Warrant.

Beech told the Metropolitan Police that he had witnessed the murder of a young boy named Scott who was "run over and killed in front of him." He claimed that Scott was a school friend who was murdered for befriending him. "It was a secret that he carried throughout his life for fear of speaking about it." The Met Police ascertained that Carol Beech was never at school with a boy named Scott. There was no missing boy. It was a complete fabrication.

Beech had 121 counselling sessions with psychotherapist Vicki Paterson. Beech sent her an e-mail with a "body map." Beech colour-coded the body map to represent injuries he claimed to have sustained. These included broken bones and wasp stings. Beech claimed that his abusers had inserted into him "various objects." Paterson testified that she was profoundly shocked at the coloured drawings but appears to have made no attempt to authenticate the veracity of Carl Beech's allegations.

Her web site is illuminating:

I will listen in a non-judgmental way understanding your world from your point of view. The starting point is to build a collaborative relationship between us which should then allow you to acknowledge and talk about your feelings, however difficult or uncomfortable they are. Working in a supportive way, emotions from the past and present will be allowed to surface and aspects of yourself.

This 'belief' is clearly problematic. No evidence came to light that Paterson implanted false memories, however, by accepting the veracity of Beech's claims uncritically, Paterson was effectively fostering his delusions. In counselling sessions with Paterson, Beech claimed that he was assaulted by a Saudi Prince and, as his delusions cemented, by a "foreign royal family." When questioned by police why he delayed reporting, Beech responded: "I did not report sooner because the group who abused me were very powerful men I have been in fear of my safety since the abuse started."

The Independent Office for Police Conduct (IOPC) declined to act against investigating officers, including the senior command team, in an investigation that cost the taxpayer over £4.5 million. Sir Bernard Howe (former head of the Met) now sits in the House of Lords. Cressida Dick, who led the original investigation into the claims of Carl Beech, was promoted to Commissioner for the Metropolitan Police; former Deputy Assistant Commissioner, Steve Rodhouse, was promoted to head of operations at the National Crime Agency. Sir Richard Henriques, a former senior High Court Judge has declared that the warrants to search the properties of the accused may have been obtained unlawfully after officers misled the court. The inquiry into the failures of Operation Midland is widely accepted by the media as a whitewash. The Henriques Report has pinpointed 43 serious police failings. Describing the operation as deeply "flawed," Henriques concluded that it was "difficult to conceive that no misconduct or criminality was involved by at least one police officer."

Former Home Secretary, David Blunkett writing in the *Daily Mail* (7 October 2019), expressed astonishment at the IOPC. "Never for a moment did I imagine such a whitewash. When I called in this newspaper two months ago for full publication of the Henriques report into Operation Midland – and that disastrous investigation by the Metropolitan police into a non-existent VIP paedophile ring – I was certain that action would follow. It did not seem remotely possible to me (that) the police complaints body could continue to ignore its findings."

Tom Watson MP

On 26 July, the Guardian newspaper published a letter by Valerie Sinason and 37 of her colleagues. They proclaimed that,

Trauma and abuse evoke powerful feelings. As therapists, psychologists, and counsellors we are concerned that the extra anger aimed at Tom Watson MP, the police and Carl Beech is missing reflection.

Tellingly, the letter did not mention Beech's many victims, nor did it make any reference to his guilty plea to possessing indecent (including Class A) images on his phone, encrypted, and hidden behind a calculator.

Tom Watson, who was later rewarded with a life peerage, met in person with Carl Beech in his Westminster office before Beech made allegations to the MET police in 2014. His Westminster statement helped fuel a moral panic about child abuse. Watson subsequently wrote to the Prime Minister insisting that a paedophile network had been operative in parliament during Margaret Thatcher's premiership. He was involved with the now discredited news agency, *Exaro*, who helped to disseminate the myth that a Westminster sex ring had operated at the heart of the Establishment. He was also in contact with police and the crown prosecution service whom he insisted ought to investigate Beech's untrue allegations. The Met police – who had previously come under fire for not taking the allegations against Jimmy Savile seriously – then set up the now discredited Operation Midland.

Daniel Janner KC, the son of the late Lord Janner, writing in the *Times* (24 January 2019) called for Watson to apologise and resign after he mis-used parliamentary privilege in proclaiming that there "was very clear intelligence" about a Westminster establishment paedophile ring. Speaking about the devastating impact of these false allegations, Janner wrote: "For six years my family has endured a living nightmare. That's how long it has been since the fantasist Carl Beech concocted his hateful series of lies about my late father, a gentle, kind and loving man who was never convicted of any offence and whose lengthy record of public service has been besmirched in the most evil way."

Grenville Janner was not the only politician besmirched by Watson. In a letter to the *Sunday Mirror* on October 2015, Lord Brittan's name was dragged through the mud. Watson wrote: "One survivor said to me that Brittan showed no kindness or warmth, and he was as close to evil as a human being could get in my view." This statement was a source of considerable distress to Brittan's family who were still reeling from the shock of his premature death from cancer four days previously. Lord Brittan would eventually be cleared after Northumbria police concluded that the allegations were baseless. Lord McDonald KC, a former director of public prosecutions, wrote in a letter to the *Times* newspaper (24 July 2019) that "politicians should never use the criminal justice system, still less particular investigations, as a way of inserting themselves into a news cycle."

2023 – TWO CASES STUDIES

Michael and Deborah

After receiving psychotherapy at a local therapy centre, Freya, accuses her grandfather and later her father. The chronological correspondence outlined below provides a snapshot into the devastating consequences on her loving family. These letters form part of a much larger file which include complaints from Freya's parents to her therapists and to Social Services. In police interview, her father described how his daughter had been brainwashed by her therapists. Significantly, following interview police declined to proceed with either complaint against Freya's father or grandfather. Both received NFA (no further action).

FAO Helen Ellis/Ms N Gregory
Trauma Group
19 September 2022

Dear Helen and Nicola

When we saw you on 26 August, you mentioned that if we wanted any more information or help to contact you. You all said how lovely it was to see us all together as a family and that it does not happen very often (editor's note: since coming into post in 2014, this is the only case in my experience where parents have participated in family 'therapy' – if that is the correct term to describe this disastrous process). Since seeing you our family unit is breaking down; we have reached a point of desperation and wondered if you can shed some light on the situation.

As you know, in 2018 we were made aware of Freya struggling at her second attempt at university being in a depressed state and carrying through destructive behaviour, alcohol, drugs, which was so upsetting to hear.

Straightaway we supported Freya; we went to the doctors, and they suggested contacting the Anniston Centre, as the waiting list on the NHS was too long and they felt she needed help immediately. She then started therapy with Dr Edwina Dawson. Freya continued to see her regularly over a four-year period. Earlier in the year Dr Dawson diagnosed Freya with PTSD and this is when Freya contacted the Trauma Group, which was selected by Freya rather than a referral. Freya then saw you, Helen. At that point you said her anxiety levels were too high for her to start PTSD treatment. You then advised her to see Nicola your mental health worker at the Trauma Group. Freya received Neuro Tapping/ Emotional Freedom Technique (EFT); Freya then started receiving sessions in "Tapping."

On returning from our holidays on 9 July, Freya told us that through tapping she had recalled "memories" of being sexually abused by her grandfather when she was seven years old. She was in a dreadful state of mind. This was a horrific revelation and incomprehensible, but we immediately sought a joint appointment with the Anniston Centre to try and make sense of the situation. The next few weeks were traumatic for her and myself and my husband, spending many sleepless nights consoling and reassuring her. For those two weeks after the first 'memory encounter' she received little support externally as Nicola went away on holiday. Over the period to date, Freya continued with some more appointments both with Anniston and the Trauma Group (currently Dr Dawon is unavailable at Anniston). She was advised by both practises to confront her alleged abuser to start 'closure and to move on.' Although we felt that this would not help her it was Freya's decision and we supported her. My husband, Michael, and her brother went with her to do this. You can imagine the devastating impact this has had on everyone across the whole of the immediate and wider family.

As we said at the meeting with you, it has been difficult for all of us and especially, Michael, since Freya has confronted her grandfather; he has now potentially lost his relationship with his mother and stepfather. Freya moved back to her ex-boyfriend as it was very apparent that all of us living together at this very raw time would not be good for her, nor us. Since then, we have kept in communication, regularly checking in with Freya, and her with us. We have tried our best to support Freya emotionally and financially as she has no income. Michael and Freya have since been to Birmingham to sort her travel visa to India and most recently Michael and Freya met for a walk. These were on the whole good positive conversations about moving forward, finding a job etc. We also finalised plans and finance of the pending India retreat trip, as it was something Freya felt she needed to do and would be helpful for her.

You can imagine our shock a few days later when she inferred that Michael had abused her in our former family home. We reported this immediately to Dr Barlow who reached out to you to communicate this and establish your opinion and Freya's state of mind. The outcome was that you said to Dr Barlow that Freya miscommunicated and was in no way accusing her father. This is certainly not the case with what she implied to Michael when he went to see Freya. This weekend she has spoken with her siblings and her brother's fiancé and has said that Michael sexually abused her. This is totally incomprehensible. The severity of this additional unfounded and untrue allegation does not only make everyone extremely sad and upset, but it adds to the damage and impact health-wise this is having on us all. It is truly catastrophic. To now include her father with these ridiculous claims indicates to us all that firstly it discredits her original allegations, but more importantly we are seriously concerned for her health and mental well-being; we are extremely worried about her ability to function. We have noticed over time that her persona has changed. This is fundamentally different from the Freya we know; she is a beautiful, bright, intelligent daughter, and we strongly believe that this therapy is not helping and in fact has damaged Freya and now her family irreversibly.

She has said she wanted to break communication with the family and have some time away for reflection, which we have respected. Within three days of saying this, she contacted her siblings and myself. She has asked if we are ok and said that she is there to support and talk, but this feels like Freya is playing us off or attempting to turn us against Michael.

We do not want Freya to feel alone but, as you can imagine, these events and the severe consequences of such are pushing us away. We all love her so much and only want the best for her. She is an adult; however, we think that she is not in a 'safe' place whatsoever. We do strongly feel that not only is she a threat to herself and people around her, but also the mental health of family members and, in particularly, my husband's wellbeing and safety is compromised.

We are not sure what she is communicating to you because the memories and behaviour she is displaying makes absolutely no sense and is so completely mis-founded, we feel that if we share our experiences then we are all joined up, and you can advise her GP accordingly. We <u>are urgently asking you</u> to review her care, and, on our part, we will again discuss with the Crisis Team, Doctor, and legal professionals.

I would like to stress this is not in anyway trying to control her, but a real dread of her harming herself and others around her.

Please can you review this letter with some urgency and respond to us directly.

Yours Sincerely

Deborah M

21 April 2023

Please tell Dad to stop. Stop these messages. Stop this blame on everyone else. Professional therapists have helped me and supported me since the day I went. All that therapy led me to the root. Yes, you are broken but I'm broken too. This is hard for us all. Yes, it is painful but listen to your daughter. I haven't been influenced by anyone else. My love hasn't changed for our family but all I want is to talk about what happened and to heal. You are talking to everyone else apart from your daughter. Please don't keep going down the route you are on and let's heal together. This is the last time I am reaching out.

Sending love and healing.

22 April 2023

Freya,

I won't tell Dad to stop! I, the family and all our closest friends believe and supported him in everything he has communicated. The police investigation into both your dad and grandfather was dismissed. The solicitors, therapists that all the family are seeing, alongside the head of Anniston have all without hesitation dismissed your stories and agree that Helen Ellis through her own tragic events validated your false memories, and we witnessed that in person which is why we have all without hesitation dismissed your stories which is why we are pursuing your therapy clinic (they are *not* professionals).

You firmly believe your thoughts, but we know the truth 100% and we all standby your grandfather and your dad and we try daily to live and love each other in the hope that one day you will realise your wrongs and return to us.

All we have is unconditional love for you, but you have chosen not to listen. What you believe is a false truth and we have no idea why. Look at your past: you had urine infections; then an insect bite on your leg; you chose to take drugs, and to self-abuse. With all these events, your dad and I, took you to the doctors and then latterly to Brookfields. We have done nothing wrong. We have loved and supported you throughout your life and if we are guilty of anything, it's giving you too much and you not standing on your own two feet. As for your 'professional therapists' at the Anniston Centre, and now this strange commune you have joined (Cult) it continues to influence you and turn you away from your family and friends. You ask Dad to stop, how can he when he is protecting his reputation, when you post your comments etc on *Facebook*, concerned friends and family quiz him and us all, we have to defend ourselves and you, because we are trying to protect you. You have chosen not to be in contact with your family and, yes, we are all broken but now we have to move on and if that's you not being in our lives, so be it.

We know 100% that nothing happened to you as a child. Hopefully, you will realise this one day. Your return to us **will be conditional** by complete retraction of the horrendous allegations against both your dad and grandfather.

We are now moving on with our lives; this is the path you have chosen – not us.

Our love, Mum, and Dad.

June 2023

Hi Freya, this is my closure letter to you.

It has been nearly a year since these unfortunate events first raised their head to your family. On returning from our holiday in Spain all our worlds have been devastated and changed dramatically.

Your initial accusations so devastating and impossible to believe impacted on all of us so enormously. When I say <u>all</u>, I also mean <u>you</u> because you so firmly believe them to be true. As parents, we took a breath, sat back and decided to support you to get to know exactly what it was or when it was that has caused such devastation to your belief in your family. From the outset back to Uni life we were there for you and supported you both as a family and seeking professional help. I now believe from other professionals that the 'help' you were given was not correct and may well have led to this. It is not unknown and in fact more common than anyone would believe that false memory exists and has ruined many families across the globe. We are just that, ruined and broken.

Our lives are shattered, and we are a strong unit that through our family and friends remain steadfast in our belief that you have been wrongly counselled and that you will one day return to our lives.

I know how badly this has affected your Mum, brother, sister, your grandparents, and extended family.

For me, I will never give up on my love for you. The hurt this has caused to me so dreadful at times I have no words to describe it. I know deep down you don't believe this either. If you truly look inward, you will see that.

You have had the most privileged upbringing and a very loving family and friendship group. So many people across the world are less fortunate. We are all very lucky people.

Over the 12 months you have missed so much that you would have shared with your family and those memories for us will be forever incomplete.

You wish me to stop blaming others, how can I when I know that I and your grandfather are not to blame? So, yes, I am resolute in blaming the 'support network' you are engaged in either past or present, and I will continue to seek justice and clear our names no matter what it costs me personally.

My health has taken a backward step and as a family we cannot relive these issues hour by hour as we do; nothing good will come from it. I have a loving family and now a beautiful granddaughter to love and care for.

<u>We choose good</u> and your Mum and I are focusing on closing the bad doors behind us and opening the good ones in front of us, and there are many.

I hope one day you will be stood there.

Until that time, you should know that the love of our daughter, Freya, is unwavering and when you realise this is a mistake and confront your misgivings, we will be there for you, and we can rebuild.

I am a Christian and my belief over the years has been tested and I lost my way with this when my father tragically died; the regrets that I have at that time were from having self-pity and been less than supportive to my wife and family. Perhaps as you link the horrendous accusations to that time, that maybe the only mistake I made is perhaps not comforting you enough, I just don't know.

I am a Christian in the belief of being kind and thankful for what I have and that I must turn away from bad and continue to promote good, strength, unity and love always.

My family is everything to me.

I'm not wanting a response unless you wish to retract all accusations and rebuild.

Go peaceful in your life. Dad x

Postscript by Michael

"Sadly, the above letter I haven't been able to send as evidently it could be seen as intimidation of a witness and I could make the situation worse for myself and my family. Daily, I live in dread of what Freya's false memories may manifest to and having read a lot about this and to what extent families have been dragged through the courts. I feel, on balance, it is better to leave alone for the wellbeing of all of us. Nevertheless, I am desperate for Freya to read this letter and this book as it might just bring her back to us. We need hope right now.

Having spent some time with Kevin, my wife and I felt compelled to be involved with this project for various reasons, but, *primarily*, to let others know that it isn't just you and others are out there; we must support each other.

This process might just have well saved us. Thank you to my wife's caring love and support, and to everyone brave enough to share their experiences, and to Kevin and his fellow professionals for compiling this life-saving publication.

Our life is forever different now, however the love from our family and friends is constant and unwavering. Let's keep moving forward, step by step."

Linda and Ronald

Following weekly psychotherapy sessions Eleanor and Michelle accuse their parents of childhood physical and sexual abuse. Linda and Ronald were later acquitted following an eight-day trial.

"We always felt we were a normal, loving, and hard-working family. Growing up both daughters were popular, with lots of friends at school. Our daughters were high achievers who later entered university, which is when things started to go spectacularly wrong, suffering with mental health issues such as depression, an eating disorder, self-harm, and anxiety.

The allegations all started after the birth of our daughters' second babies; one daughter was diagnosed-with Post Natal Depression (PND). She was prescribed anti-depressants and referred to a therapist. Almost immediately she came to me saying she had felt "uncomfortable" when we cuddled on the couch during childhood, after bath time and before bedtime. I was horrified to say the least.

As the months progressed our daughter was having weekly sessions with her therapist. She developed further "bad feelings" about her childhood. After counselling sessions, she would have "dreams" and "flashbacks" and looked to myself at first for answers. As the "dreams" developed, so did the allegations. Her sister, who had given birth to her second baby, started therapy some six months later. Initially, the second daughter made it very clear she did not recall *any* childhood abuse. However, she too very quickly made allegations, initially against her father. Our older son has never shared his sister's "memories."

A Child Protection Concern was then raised with Social Services (SS). At this time, I looked after my Grandchildren and worked with children in a professional capacity. An investigation was undertaken by SS, yet they and the police declined to take the case forward. I quickly returned to work, although it was disclosed that my daughter's therapist had deemed the "cuddling" as sexual abuse.

Matters escalated, however as my daughter's false memories developed. My husband and I were later arrested and charged with 11 counts, including attempted rape. I lost my career in social work, being forced to resign. My husband was supported

by his employer to return to work when he was strong enough. He continued in his job until after the trial before retiring. I continue to be extremely proud of him to have managed that. This gave me the strength to face every day.
To the family and good friends who stood shoulder to shoulder with us, I don't think we would have survived without you!

At the time my husband was accused, I became suicidal and made one real attempt on my life. I finally found the strength to fight after I was re-arrested later in 2020, as our daughters continued to make statements to police. I found the British False Memory Society. That was when things started to change. I became proactive in our defence. I began reading about False Memory, (14 books to date) and we received constant support from the Society throughout this process, prior to facing the terrifying prospect of an eight-day criminal trial.

It took three years to get to trial where we were both acquitted of the sexual allegations; I was found not guilty of physical assault charges. I firmly believe the outcome would have been so different without the commitment and unswerving support of the BFMS and we will be forever in their debt.

Nine months later, we are trying to adjust. We feel grateful not to have the threat of potential imprisonment hanging over us and feel more hopeful for the future. Yet the grief and heartbreak of our hitherto beautiful family being torn apart remains.

I do allow myself some anger at the therapists who were not called to court to be held accountable and both continue to practice today. However, this will not destroy me, and my hope is my beautiful family will one day return to the nest. Recently I have drafted the following letter to our daughter's therapists."

MEMORY & INJUSTICE

Dear Therapist,

September 2023

I feel compelled to write to you on behalf of myself and my husband to put into words the absolute heartbreak your therapy has caused to our beautiful daughters and to our whole family.

Our vulnerable daughter, Michelle, became your client after your colleague, Anita Smith, encouraged her client, our daughter Eleanor, to "get her sister to Therapy." Both daughters were vulnerable and entered counselling following post-natal depression and, as you are aware, they were prescribed medication to help ameliorate depression.

Through you and your joint methods, which included dream interpretation, leading to "flashbacks," our daughters steadily deteriorated and developed false memories of childhood abuse. These so-called flashbacks helped create false and distorted memories about our daughter's loving and normal childhood.

Michelle's sister started therapy some six months earlier and she claimed to be experiencing "bad feelings" and dreams that something bad may have happened to her in childhood following counselling sessions with Anita Smith.

Michelle said she did not have these thoughts. However, within two to three sessions, she "recovered memories" of her father allegedly abusing her some 25 years earlier. How were these therapeutically driven claims even possible? Eleanor began to have dreams and flashbacks which would become more vivid in detail as the sessions with you continued.

I believe therapists are warned of the dangers of inducing false memories by using such methods (which in this instance sounds worryingly like hypnosis) as there has been no independent scientific evidence to support the existence of recovered memories despite over 30 years of scientific research into the subject. Indeed, it is widely documented and accepted by the mainstream scientific community that trauma is more likely to be remembered, than forgotten. Are we to believe that both our daughters buried these memories and you both magically unlocked their minds? Even now it sounds incredulous.

My husband and I believe you set out to "look" for historical abuse from the outset even though Eleanor told you and others this had not happened to her. I became aware that you and Michelle's therapist were colleagues at this time, and we still feel that this was a conflict of interest. Michelle would have a session on a Monday and Eleanor on a Wednesday. They certainly swapped notes, and their recollections became contaminated. I guess we will never know as both you and your colleague were never compelled to attend court to be held accountable for your practice.

My Husband and I may not have any redress with you, however, one day our daughters will "work out" what happened to them during therapy with you and want you to be held accountable for your part in our family's destruction!

The pain and destruction that has been caused to our daughters and the whole family is truly catastrophic. We have been dragged through the criminal justice system. Our previous loving and close family remains fractured. Our daughters are estranged. Our Grandchildren were fully in our lives until therapy and Michelle made you aware that "I was the safest person with her children." Did you not stop to listen to this? Michelle also shared with you that she was concerned about the relationship between Eleanor and her therapist and felt this was "unhealthy" with her therapist holding "too much power" over her. I wonder if you recorded these concerns or ever acted on them! These were shared at the beginning of Michelle's therapy with you.

Our door remains open to our daughters in the hope that one day they might come back to us. We are innocent of these heinous crimes and continue to suffer every day because of the dubious therapeutic methods used on our daughters. We have hope that one day you will be compelled to give a clear and open account of your practice. Until then, it is a real concern for clients and their families if these methods continue to be used in their "treatment." The damage to our daughter continues.

We don't believe you ever intended to cause harm; however, you need to hear that harm is what was caused in a catastrophic way that may never be rectified. That is the real tragedy.

Mrs Linda and Mr Ronald A

Editor's Note – In early 2023, I attended trial to observe the defence case for Linda and Ronald. The atmosphere in court was tense although not as tense as sitting in the public area awaiting the jury's deliberations. Unusually the complainants abuse 'memories' featured strongly as the evidence unfolded. The erudite legal teams were alive to the possibility of false memories and in consequence two memory experts were instructed by the defence. Their reports were based on the evidence and scientific literature on the study of human memory. One of the reports was not admitted into evidence. The defence did call as an expert witness a psychology professor, a practising consultant forensic psychologist. The professor testified that he had previously written over 200 expert reports on the scientific nature of human memory. He has given evidence in the Supreme Court and in the Criminal Court of Appeal. The professor testified that memory does not work like a video recorder or a filing cabinet. He gave detailed testimony about the science of memory citing the Brandon Report on recovered memories of childhood sexual abuse published in the *British Journal of Psychiatry* (April 1998, Vol 172, pp. 296 – 307) and its implications for clinical practice. Detailed reference was made to the Research Board of the British Psychological Society whose revised *Guidelines on Memory and the Law* were published in 2010. Here are some of the key findings which were put to the court:

Memories are records of people's experiences of events and are not a record of the events themselves. In this respect, they are unlike other recording media such as videos or audio recordings, to which they should not be compared.

Memory is not only of experienced events, but it is also of the knowledge of a person's life, i.e., schools, occupations, holidays, friends, homes, achievements, failures tec. As a general rule memory is more likely to be accurate when it is of the knowledge of a person's life than when it is of specific experienced events.

Remembering is a reconstructive process. Memories are mental constructions that bring together different types of knowledge in an act of remembering. As a consequence, memory is prone to error and is easily influenced by the recall environment, including police interviews and cross-examination in court.

Memories for experienced events are always incomplete. Memories are time-compressed fragmentary records of experience. Any account of a memory will feature forgotten details and gaps, and this must not be taken as any sort of indicator of accuracy. Accounts of memories that do not feature forgetting and gaps are highly unusual.

Memories typically contain only a few highly specific details. Detailed recollection of the specific time and date of experiences is normally poor, as is highly specific information such as the precise recall of spoken conversations. As a general rule, a high degree of very specific detail in a long-term memory is unusual.

Recall of a single or several highly specific details does not guarantee that a memory is accurate or even that it actually occurred. In general, the only way to establish the truth of a memory is with independent corroborating evidence.

The content of memories arises from an individual's comprehension of an experience, both conscious and non-conscious. This content can be further modified and changed by subsequent recall.

People can remember events that they have not in reality experienced. This does not necessarily entail deliberate deception. For example, an event that was imagined, was a blend of a number of different events, or that makes personal sense for some or other reason, can come to be genuinely experienced as a memory (these are often referred to as 'confabulations').

Memories for traumatic experienced, childhood events, interview and identification practices, memory in younger children and older adults and other vulnerable groups all have special features. These are features that are unlikely to be commonly known to a non-expert, but about which an appropriate memory expert will be able to advise a court.

The jury observed intensively while the professor gave evidence; several jury members were taking notes. You could hear a pin drop. I have attended court in civil and criminal (mostly) proceedings on 43 separate occasions since coming into post in 2014, but I have never observed such detailed testimony in a case where false memories were suspected. Following cross examination, the jury retired on Thursday afternoon. The following day, at 4. 00 pm, there was a Tannoy announcement. The jury had reached verdicts on each count. Linda and Ron embraced before entering court. It was terrifying. Thankfully, the jury returned not guilty verdicts.

# THE CASELOAD OF THE BRITISH FALSE MEMORY SOCIETY

PREFACE

'Be Prepared.'

By Claire Anderson (Solicitor.)

As a Criminal Defence Solicitor practicing for over 30 years I have represented hundreds of clients at police interview in respect of a huge variety of offences ranging from low level theft to murder, complex fraud and all manner of offences of a sexual nature.

My advice isn't generic. It is tailored to the specific facts of a particular case and my advice to my client will depend on several factors including the amount of pre interview disclosure provided by the interviewing officer (this varies significantly from case to case), the quality of the instruction provided by my client and the personal characteristics of the client themselves.

The starting point for all of my advice is an explanation of the police caution read to the interviewee by the officer at the outset of the interview. A bit of a mouthful but it goes like this:

"You do not have to say anything, but it may harm your defence if you fail to mention, when questioned, something which you later rely on at Court. Anything you do say may be given in evidence."

So, in short, you DO have the right to silence when questioned under caution (there are exceptions in certain terrorist cases) however that right is qualified by the warning that failing to raise a defence in interview, then relying on that defence at trial risks the jury or determining Magistrate, depending on where you are tried, being permitted to consider the reasons for your silence at the early interview stage and the reason they may attribute to that silence is guilt.

Generally, there are 3 routes to go down in interview:

a. Make 'no comment' to all questions put.

b. Submit a written statement prepared from your instructions by your solicitor outlining the salient points of your defence, then answer "no comment" to all questions.

c. Answer all questions in full.

Option (a) is advice I may give if I consider that evidentially there is insufficient evidence to charge my client. It may be that the police are conducting a 'fishing expedition' ie attempting to obtain information from the interviewee to perhaps use against another party. Alternatively, it may be that the allegation is that of an old and complex fraud and the client cannot be expected to comment properly on events involving paper transactions that occurred many years before without access to particular documentation.

I may advise No Comment where the client cannot offer any defence however consider that for tactical reasons an early confession is not beneficial. As you can imagine, however the police generally assume that where a no comment interview takes place it is because the suspect has something to hide. This is NOT, however, how the court will necessarily approach this situation. Sometimes the advising lawyer at the interview will give evidence at trial providing reasons for the advice. This can avert any negative inference being drawn.

Option (b) is an extremely useful strategy that allows inferences to be minimised or even avoided but protects the client from scrutiny that may lead to self-incrimination or the incrimination of co-suspects. Additionally, I may advise this course if my client is mentally or emotionally vulnerable. A prepared statement allows the lawyer and client to exercise some control over the interview process.

Option (c) is always a bit risky but frankly any defence lawyer will tell you that an interview where the suspect answers all questions put in a convincing and comprehensive manner is a very good start to defending a prosecuted case. It may very well also avoid charge as information provided can give the police facts that point away from guilt. This route does rely on proper police disclosure, and a client confident enough to feel they can stand up to scrutiny. Being accused of a crime (especially a sexual offence) and being questioned by an officer who on occasion displays bias, is not a walk in the park.

A historic sex allegation is the one offence where I very rarely advise a no comment interview. I often assume conduct of cases that are prosecuted where another firm has dealt with the matter at police station stage. I am sometimes baffled at the quality of the advice provided. A client may come to me full of denial and with pertinent information that could have been followed up by police at an early stage but were advised by their then solicitor that as the case was old, and was based on one person's testimony only, the case was weak and so making "no comment" was appropriate. Make no mistake, a defendant CAN be convicted by a jury on the word of one complainant only however long ago the alleged offences took place. This astonishes many clients to learn, however a sex act is not ordinarily committed in front of an audience so offences like these fall into a category of their own.

The majority of my clients requested to attend an interview after a historic sexual allegation has been reported do so as a 'volunteer.' This means they are not arrested as such but are entitled to a lawyer. The vast majority of my clients are very keen to deny the allegations made and can sometimes produce documentation that may undermine the testimony of the accuser. I have for example represented people who can produce birthday cards containing loving messages from their accuser or e mails and texts that by their nature undermine the complainant's credibility.

If you are accused, seek out any such documentation. In potential false memory cases try and provide as much information as possible regarding pre and post therapy behaviour. It may be that the 'loving' messages stopped abruptly post therapy. All of the things are very important to disclose, if possible, at investigation stage.

The Police are there to investigate, not judge. However, unfortunately some officers cannot help but present as Prosecutor in interview. Recently I represented a male adult interviewed in what may well be a false memory case. He gave robust and detailed responses in the interview, however the officer questioning him assumed the role of the complainant's 'therapist' and seemed determined to persuade the interviewee to allow the accuser 'closure' by making admissions. Her questions were unfair and inappropriate, and I naturally interjected several times to voice my objections only to be threatened with removal from the interview! I wasn't removed, however. If the client had gone unrepresented, he would have struggled to cope with the ridiculous questions he was being asked to answer.

The bottom line here is that if you or a loved one are required to attend a police interview, ensure you engage a lawyer experienced in dealing with sexual offences. Seek out potentially helpful paperwork and show this to your lawyer before the interview.

You are only likely to be interviewed once before an outcome decision is made, so make it a good one and BE PREPARED.

Below is an early draft of an academic paper written in 2022 by Dr Lawrence Patihis and Dr Kevin Felstead. A revised manuscript will be published subsequently in a Special Edition of the Journal of Legal and Criminological Psychology.

Abstract

The British False Memory Society (BFMS) is a registered charity founded in 1993 following an epidemic of false memory-type accusations by adult accusers who claimed to have remembered childhood sexual abuse for which they previously had no cognitive recollection. Most of these accusers had entered counselling after typically suffering from anxiety, depression, and relationship problems. Many came out of therapy with what appeared to be false memories, and the accused sometimes contacted the BFMS for advice and support. Since its inception, the BFMS has kept a record of all calls to its telephone helpline. In this article, we document several caseload details by year from 1993 onwards. In the peak year of 1994, 268 cases were taken on by the BFMS. During recent years the number of cases taken on by the BFMS oscillated around about 40 each year. The 2010s had just 3% of total cases leading to guilty verdict (1990s = 8%; 2000s = 17%). We found the 2000 decade to be the most likely for those accused to be convicted, and the most recent years the least. We conclude that although the numbers have lessened since the 1994 peak, there are still a lot of individuals being affected by false memory type allegations today.

British False Memory Society: Caseload and Details by Year (1993 Onwards)

The debate about repressed memories of childhood abuse appears to continue, as indeed the practice of recovering memories in therapy appears to still occur. The 1980s saw an apparent increase of false memory production in recovered memory therapies, whilst this continued in the 1990s where the debate about repressed memories came to the fore in the so-called memory wars (Crews, 1995). Patihis et al. (2014) found some evidence that in the last decade sufficient numbers of the public and therapists still believe in repressed memory to sustain a supply and demand for recovered memory therapy. Patihis and Pendergrast (2019) then revealed that recovering repressed memories in therapy was still being reported by some of the public even in those beginning therapy in recent years. Patihis and Pendergrast also found data to suggest there was a peak in the 1990s of repressed memory cases. Given the apparent peak in the 1990s but nevertheless evidence of a sustained current continuation of repressed memory beliefs and practice, we wondered what patterns we would find in a charity dealing with such accusations. The BFMS is a UK-based charity that helps clients who appear to be falsely accused where recovered memories are suspected. In the current article, we look to the archives of the BFMS to see how caseloads of potential false memory accusations involving repressed memories have changed year by year since 1993.

Although the narrative typically posits a decrease of repressed memory cases both in legal cases and in wider society, some have argued that belief in unconscious repression in the UK, the US, and throughout parts of western Europe, appears to continue (Pendergrast, 2017; Shaw & Vredeveldt, 2019) or may have even increased by some measures (Otgaar et al, 2019). Otgaar et al (2021) reviewed past research and reported that belief in unconscious repression is prevalent in clinical, legal, and academic settings. It is in this context of not being sure that the phenomena declined, or whether it is in resurgence, that it will be interesting to track other measures of repressed memory legal cases over time.

One central part of this debate is the potential harm done to individuals, not only in terms of those that come to believe false memories of trauma, but also those that subsequently are falsely accused. Repressed memory beliefs and practices can lead to false accusations, and if left unchallenged in a criminal court can lead to miscarriages of justice (Gudjonsson, 1997c; Burgoyne and Brand; 2010; Burnett; 2016) and to significant family breakdown (Brand, 2007; Howe *et al*; 2018 Maran, 2010).

Past Research on the British False Memory Society

There have been a few research projects documenting some aspects of the BFMS in the 1990s, and some limited work since. Gudjonsson (1997a, 1997b) conducted a survey of BFMS members in 1995 when the total BMFS current membership was at 403 people, and of those 282 questionnaires were completed. The accusations had several consequences. About 59% of the families had lost contact with the accusing person, with 41% maintaining only "some" contact. Almost a third of the accused had sought psychological treatment because of the accusations. Perhaps most relevant to the statistics reported in the current study, Gudjonsson found that 26% of the accusations had been reported to police, with 14% ($n = 37$) reporting that criminal proceedings had been instigated.

A follow-up study (Gudjonsson, 1997c) with the same dataset of BFMS members examined the 37 cases that had criminal legal proceedings instigated. Gudjonsson found that 23 (62%) of the defendants were charged by the police. Three of these 23 cases were subsequently discontinued by the Crown Prosecution Service, while 20 proceeded to court. Out of these 20 proceeding to court, eight cases resulted in a conviction and a lengthy prison sentence. These eight convictions equated to 22% out of the 37 cases in which a criminal investigation was started, and 3% of the total number of BMFS questionnaires completed (282).

In a more recent analysis of the BFMS paper archival records, reported in a conference paper presentation Shaw et al. (2017) examined a sample of 257 cases. They found most accusations involved a single accuser and a single accused individual, with biological fathers the most likely to be accused. For more on some qualitative background information on the BFMS see Brand (2007), Burgoyne and Brand (2010), Felstead and French (2022). These past papers reveal a few gaps in the literature: there has been no peer reviewed journal article in recent years documenting BFMS cases, and there has been no update on the Gudjonsson articles of the 1990s. Perhaps most notable is the lack of prior research documenting longitudinal trends in cases over time.

The Present Study

The present study is, to our knowledge, the first of its kind to track the longitudinal progression of cases in a false memory organization over decades. Gudjonsson's (1997a, 1997b, 1997c) articles gave us a snapshot of BFMS cases in 1995, and Shaw et al (2017) gave a snapshot more recently in a conference paper. Here, we examine the BFMS caseload to track how new cases, police involvement, and guilty verdicts have changed over the years.

Method

The following data was extracted by the second author from paper records of telephone calls with individuals who contacted the BFMS helpline. A telephone information data sheet was filled out by the person taking the call at the time of the call. The telephone information sheet (TIS) has stayed approximately the same from 1993 to the present day. Note when emails were the first point of contact, a telephone call was arranged, and almost all the initial filling out of the TIS were completed via the telephone. The BFMS case worker sometimes would later update the telephone information sheet as the case progressed – for example if police became involved later or if some other information was provided via the telephone helpline that belonged on the sheet.

Following a telephone interview, a decision was made to take on a case with the BFMS, or not. If the case appeared to not involve false memories, the case was usually not taken and instead the BFMS would recommend a defence solicitor. In general, the BFMS only accepted a case if there were 'red flags' that might indicate a false memory. Those red flags included their accusers claiming to have recovered memories following counselling sessions for an adult problem, such as anxiety or depression. Another red flag was that the accusers had no memory of past child abuse prior to entering therapy. A period of not knowing about the abuse followed by a vivid memory recovery in therapy was another red flag.

The second author coded several variables from the BFMS archives from the 1993 files onwards:

Year

This was coded from the original date on the telephone information data sheet. In other words, the year in this study refers to the year the case was first reported to the BFMS.

New Cases

This variable is the actual number of cases selected by the BFMS, after the screening process.

Police Involved Cases

This variable is the subset of new cases in which the police had contacted the accused to inform him/her of the accusations.

Found Guilty

This variable is the subset of police involved cases in which the accused was found guilty.

Crown Court Trials Since 2015

The information we report on crown court trials since 2015 was collected by the second author from the BFMS files. The second author began work at the BFMS in 2014 and helped document these cases, as well as compile some data for this study.

Results

Table 1 documents the number of new cases taken on by the BFMS, the number of those cases in which a police investigation had been started, and the number of these cases in which the accused was found guilty.

Year	Number of new cases	Police involved	Found guilty	% of new cases police involved	% of police involved found guilty	% of new cases found guilty
1993	**260**	35	10	13.5	28.6	3.8
1994	**268**	60	12	22.4	20	4.5
1995	131	33	4	25.2	12.1	3.1
1996	86	28	9	32.6	32.1	10.5
1997	185	58	12	31.4	20.7	6.5
1998	162	60	15	37	25	9.3
1999	124	**69**	**30**	55.6	**43.5**	**24.2**
2000	96	54	23	56.3	42.6	**24**
2001	103	62	21	**60.2**	33.9	20.4
2002	105	62	18	**59**	29	17.1
2003	134	**67**	**29**	50	**43.3**	21.6
2004	74	39	9	52.7	23.1	12.2
2005	50	29	6	58	20.7	12
2006	41	19	7	46.3	36.8	17.1
2007	40	13	5	32.5	38.5	12.5
2008	42	17	3	40.5	17.6	7.1
2009	35	20	4	57.1	20	11.4
2010	40	10	1	25	10	2.5
2011	31	8	2	25.8	25	6.5
2012	30*	16	1	53.3	6.3	3.3
2013	34	8	0*	23.5	0.0*	0.0*
2014	31*	10	0*	32.3	0.0*	0.0*
2015	31*	7	0*	22.6	0.0*	0.0*
2016	43	10	0*	23.3	0.0*	0.0*
2017	37	12	4	32.4	33.3	10.8
2018	37	8	1	21.6	12.5	2.7
2019	36	4*	0*	11.1*	0.0*	0.0*
2020	33	4*	0*	12.1	0.0*	0.0*
2021	45	14	1	31.1	7.1	2.2
Total	2364	836	227	35.4	27.2	9.6

Table 1.

Table 1. By year, of first reporting to the BFMS, the number of new cases taken on, number of those cases which involved a police investigation, and the number found guilty.

Note. **Bolded** in Table 1 are the two years with the highest number of the given variable. *The two years (or more for ties) with the lowest number of the given variable.

In Figure 1 we document the number of new cases that were taken on by the BFMS every year since 1993. As you can see, there was a peak of a couple of hundred in some years in the 1990s, and in more recent years the numbers vary around about 40 new cases each year.

Number of new cases

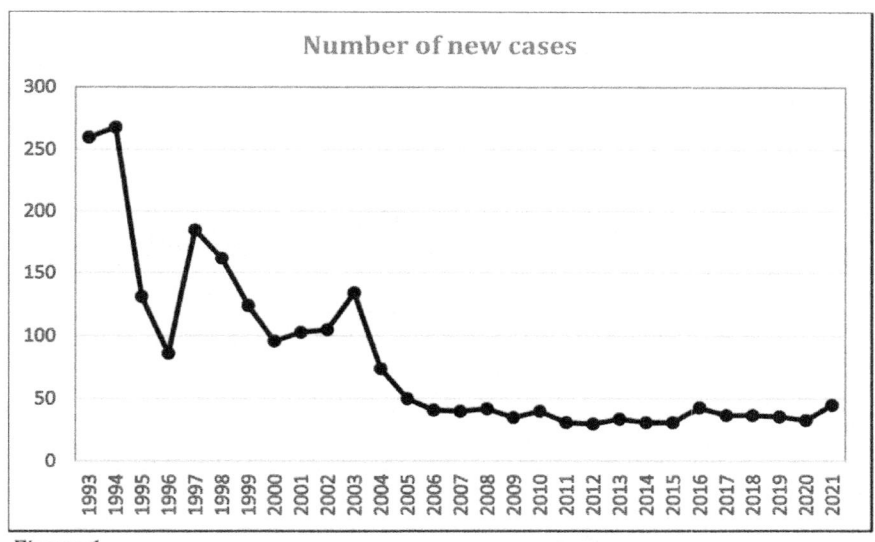

Figure 1.

These are the number of cases that were selected at the interview stage to be taken on by the BFMS. As seen in Figure 2 the number of cases taken on by the BFMS that had police involvement has in some years been as high as 50 and 60 per year, and those peaks occurred in some years in the 1990s and 2000s. As seen in the graph, in the most recent decade, this number has fluctuated around 10 per year.

Figure 2 shows the percentage of police involved cases as a

percentage of the total number of new cases taken on by the BFMS over a given year. This graph shape is less clear but appears to indicate a higher percentage of cases resulting in police involvement in the 2000s, with a smaller proportion before and since then.

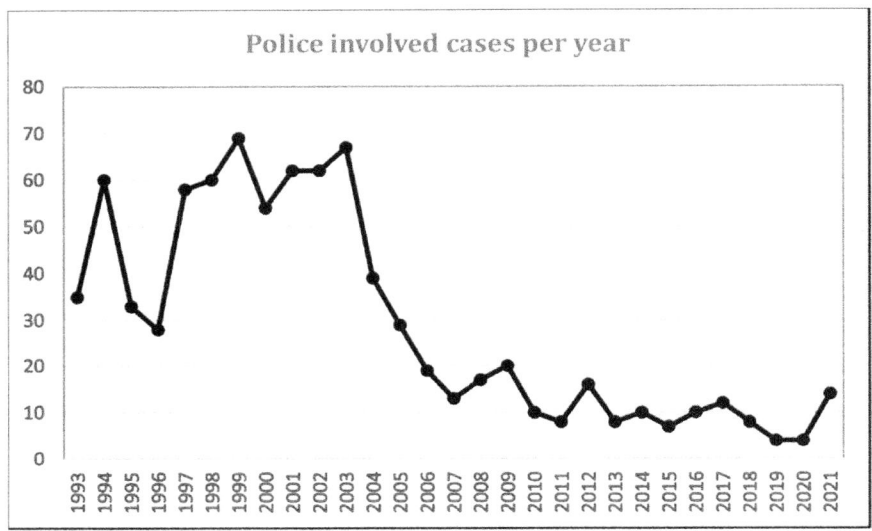

Figure 2.

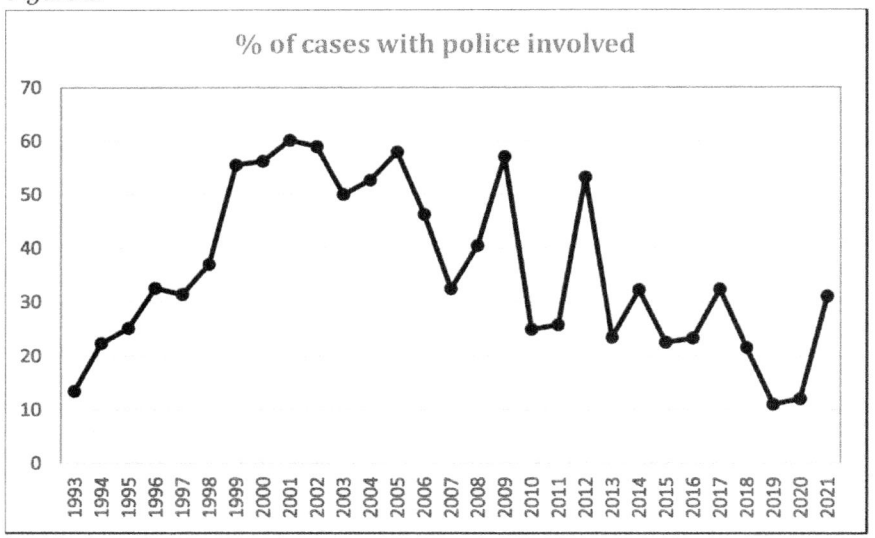

Figure 3.

Figure 3 The percentage of total BFMS cases per year that involved the police.

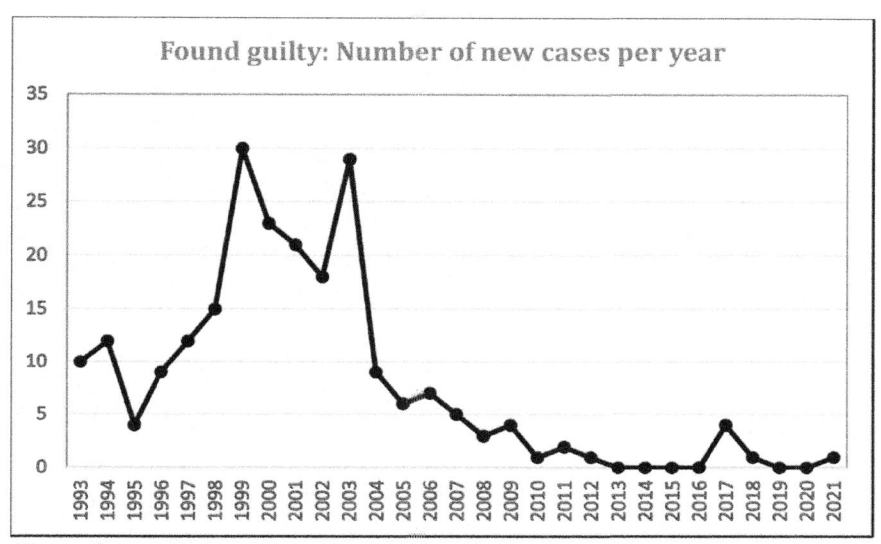

[Figure 4: Line graph titled "Found guilty: Number of new cases per year" showing values from 1993 to 2021, with peaks around 1999 (30) and 2003 (29), declining to near 0 in recent years.]

Figure 4.

Figure 4 shows the number of BFMS cases in which the defendant was found guilty. Here, we see in terms of raw numbers, this was highest in 1999 and 2003, and in recent years very few have been found guilty. Figure 5 shows these guilty verdicts as a percentage of the number of police-involved cases the BFMS was dealing with each year. This graph therefore documents the approximate likelihood that if a case involved a police investigation it would result in a guilty verdict at the conclusion of that investigation. This graph shows a different shape, though we still see peaks in 1999 and 2003.

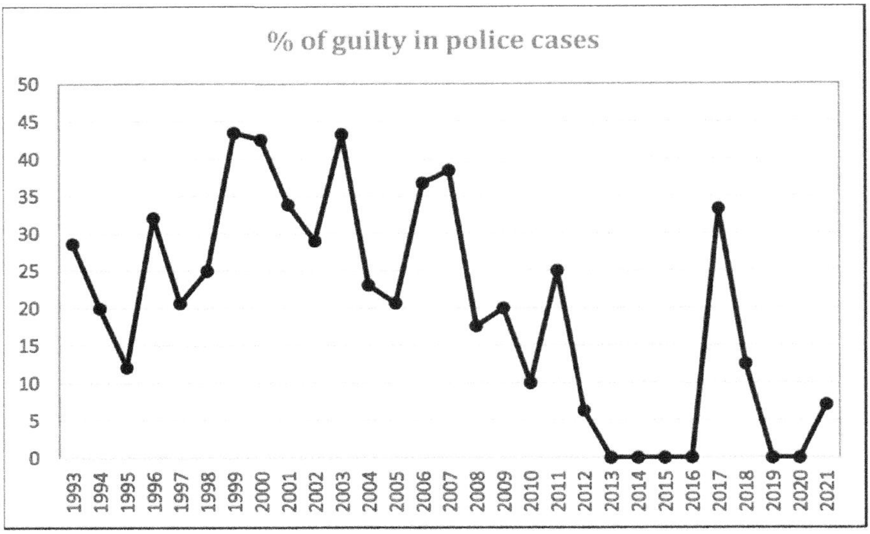

Figure 5.

Figure 5. The number of BFMS cases per year that resulted in the defendant being found guilty of the allegation. Percentage of BFMS police-involved cases in which the defendant was found not guilty. The denominator in this graph is the number of police-involved cases taken on by the BFMS each year.

Figure 6, documents the percentage found guilty out of the total new cases taken on in a given year by the BFMS. This therefore approximately illustrates the likelihood that a case taken on by the BFMS would result in a guilty verdict later.

% of new cases found guilty

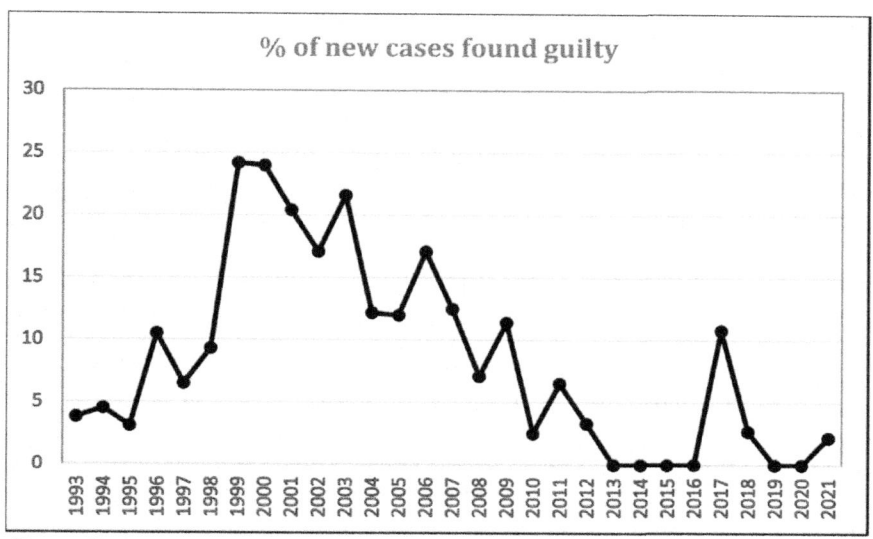

Figure 6.

Figure 6. The percentage of cases found guilty per year. The denominator in this graph is the total number of new cases taken on by the BFMS each year.

Further Analyses by Multiyear Time Periods

Table 2 below documents the percentage of cases that led to a guilty verdict for each decade. The decade that a new case was most likely to result in a guilty verdict was the 2000s, and the decade least likely was the 2010s (with as yet insufficient data for the 2020 decade).

Decade	Percentage of cases found guilty
1990s (1993–1999)	7.6%
2000s (2000–2009)	17.4%
2010s (2010–2019)	2.6%
2020s (2020–2021)	1.3%*

Table 2. Decade comparisons of percentage of cases that resulted in guilty verdicts.

Note. *Only two years' worth of data and eight cases are ongoing from the 2020/2021, so it is too early to conclude any trend for this current decade. None of the cases in the earlier decades, including the 2010s, are ongoing in regard to current legal investigations.

If we examine shorter multiyear periods to investigate apparent patterns, we found in the period from 1993–1998, 5.7% (n = 62 of 1092 cases) of BFMS members were convicted at trial. From 1999–2003, 21.5% of cases resulted in conviction (n = 121 of 562). From 2004–2010, out of a caseload of 322, 10.9% resulted in conviction (n = 35). During the decade from 2011 – 2021, out of a total of 388 cases, there was a conviction rate in 9.1% of cases (n = 9). In total, 227 members of the BFMS were convicted at trial.

Crown Court Trials Since 2015

Since 2014, BFMS accused members have appeared in 11 crown court trials, resulting in a conviction rate of 41.7% (n = 5) for those that went to trial. In the period from 2014 – 2021, 43 accused BFMS members who were interviewed by police were not prosecuted ("no further action" cases).

Discussion

The main findings of this study are that the number of new cases taken on by the BFMS has declined from more than 200 at peak years in the 1990s (1993 and 1994) to a still meaningful 40 per year in the last 10 years. Perhaps surprisingly the peak years for the number of new cases in which the police had started an investigation was in the early 2000s. Similarly, the early 2000s also documented peaks for the percentage of cases found guilty, and this pattern was found when this percentage was per total cases taken on, and per cases involving a police investigation. Interestingly, the decade with the lowest guilty verdict percentage was the most recent—the 2010s had just 3% of total cases leading to a guilty verdict (17% in the 2000s; 8% in the 1990s). These patterns are slightly different to the standard narrative of the progression of recovered memory cases – the standard narrative being of a peak in the 1990s and reducing numbers in 2000 decade. We found the 2000 decade to be the most vulnerable to those accused, and the most recent 2010 the least vulnerable for those accused via recovered memory accusations.

If we compare our data to Gudjonsson's (1997a, b, c) data he collected in 1995, we are reassured to see we found similar numbers for that year – by a very different method. For example, Gudjonsson found that in 1995, 22% of cases in which a criminal investigation was started resulted in a conviction, while we found 25%. Gudjonsson found 3% of the total number of BMFS questionnaires completed were found guilty in his 1995 dataset, we found 3% too for 1995. This is encouraging because in Gudjonsson (1997, a, b, c) he derived his data from questionnaires, while we used the more direct source of the actual BFMS files. The fact that we got similar numbers with different methods could mean both datasets have some measure of accuracy (although there is the possibility of a systematic error affecting both datasets).

The upward trend in the percentage of cases resulting in convictions increasing from 6% in the 1993–1998 to 22% in the 1999–2003 period is difficult to explain. Legislative changes may be of some relevance. Prior to 1994, judges were required to give a mandatory corroboration ruling during rape trials. This was removed under the Criminal Justice and Public Order Act 1994 (Elliot & Quinn, 2000). Significantly, the right to remain silent during police interviews was also curtailed in 1994.

Though this does not map onto our dates exactly, it is possible that these legislative changes, in particular the removal of the mandatory corroboration warning, impacted on future cases. The peak of guilty findings in 2003 appears to coincide with the Sexual Offences Act (2003) which most likely raised awareness about sexual abuse but the extent to which police, the crown prosecution service, and juries were more aware of sexual abuse and more likely to prosecute and convict is unknown. Conviction rates underwent a gradual decline thereafter.

The most recent decade was the most successful for reducing the number of cases that go on to have guilty verdicts. There were no convictions in 2013, 2014, 2015, 2016, 2019 and 2020. There were three convictions in 2017, and one conviction in 2018 and in 2021. It may be of significance that in 2017 and 2018, and 2021 the accused contacted the BFMS relatively late – when legal proceedings were already advanced. From the second author's perspective, some of these legal teams were inexperienced in dealing with false-memory-type accusations. The first author speculates that the BFMS may have become more skilled in dealing with false allegations as the years have progressed. Perhaps a partial cause of this is that the BFMS has recently identified several rules for the falsely accused, which include act fast, make records, create a timeline, immediately see a solicitor, actively prepare a defence (see the preface to this chapter).

The 40 cases or so per year in recent years is significant. Britain is a relatively small country, and these cases likely represent just the tip of the iceberg of other repressed memory cases occurring in the country. It may be that many false memory cases that occur in therapy are not reported to the BFMS. Those cases that do not involve forthright allegations may never be understood enough by the accused to know whether false memories were involved. Cases that do not involve the police might also be less likely to be reported to the BFMS. In addition, some of the falsely accused in recovered memory scenarios may not know about the BFMS. Some may be too embarrassed to contact the BFMS. Better education on the topic of false memories in the public, clinical psychology, and legal professionals may be identifying false memory cases without need to consult with the BFMS. Nevertheless, we speculate that the number of families suffering tremendously from emotional pain and estrangement because of false memories in psychotherapies is likely much higher than 40 new cases per year. Of course, the suffering is cumulative: it is being added to by at least forty per year; many 1990s false memory cases are still causing great sorrow still today, with some of the falsely accused in their 80s and still seeking to connect again with their estranged daughters (mostly). The BFMS also provides moral support in such older cases on an ongoing basis, even when there is no longer a legal threat.

The data presented in this article supplies just a fragmentary glimpse into the reality of false memory-type allegations. From the second authors' experience helping those accused of false events recovered through therapy, there is an almost immeasurable, catastrophic footprint left on one's life following a false accusation. The waiting period prior to a police interview is extremely stressful. Being handcuffed in front of your family, taken to the police station, and locked in a cell is horrific. Released whilst 'under investigation' is psychologically stressful. The length of cases as they drag on for months or years is a chronic stressor for many. The accused often remain under investigation for 6 months, 12 months, or longer. Another harrowing aspect of these cases is, in addition to a police investigation, the involvement of Social Services.

There are some limitations to this study. There are other variables in the BFMS archive that could possibly have been coded given more time. The time taken coding decades of cases, thousands of files, with each file having not only a telephone information sheet, but other documents, was challenging for four variables and may be very difficult for even more variables. One variable that was not coded and would have been very difficult to code are cases that were not selected (or taken on) by the BFMS. We coded what we judged to be the variables of most interest. Of course, some inaccuracies may creep into both the coding and the original file keeping, but we were glad to see some convergence with Gudjonsson's 1995 data (1997a, b, c).

Though declining over time, these allegations emerging primarily from accusers who did not know they were abused before entering therapy are still catastrophic for the accused. We suspect false memories in many of these cases due to the red flags discussed earlier. We speculate that the accused are innocent. The resulting loss of reputation, family breakdown, and wrongful incarceration (Burnett, 2016) is a heavy burden for many still today. The caseload of the BFMS has declined over time, however accusations based on false memory-type allegations, recovered in therapy, remain a real and serious issue in the UK. These wrongful accusations continue to damage society and dilute attention away from cases involving real abuse. There is a need for false memories to be better understood by criminal justice professionals, clinicians, juries, and the public. The false dichotomy of allegations being seen as either truth or lies needs to change to one that acknowledges false memories as a reasonable option (Shaw et al., 2017). The evidence from this study suggests that we are a long way from achieving this goal.

Dr Lawrence Patihis is a Senior Lecturer in Pschology at the University of Portsmouth.

He is the author of Trauma, Memory, and Law: Lectures on repressed memories, memory distortions, and trauma (Amazon KDP. 2nd edition, 2023).

Dr Kevin Felstead was the director of communications, BFMS from 2014 – 2023.

He is the author of Justice for Carol: the Creation of a Satanic Myth in the UK (Felstead and Felstead, Create Space Independent Publishing Platform, 2014).

REFERENCES

Brand, N. (Ed). (2007). Fractured Families: The anguish of the falsely accused. Bradford on Avon: The British False Memory Society.

Brooknan, F. & Robinson, A. (2012. Violent Crime, 564 – 594. The Oxford Handbook of Criminology (fifth edition). Oxford University Press

Burgoyne, W., & Brand, N. (2010). Miscarriage of Memory: Historic abuse cases – a dilemma for the legal system. Bradford on Avon: British False Memory Society.

Burnett, R. (2016). Wrongful Allegations of sexual and child abuse. Oxford University Press.

Crews (1995). The Memory Wars: Freud's Legacy in Dispute. The New York Review of Books.

Elliot, C., & Quinn, F. (2000), Criminal Law. Pearson Education

Limited. Essex, England.

Felstead, K., & French, C. C. (2022). Dr James Ost's contributions to the work of the British false memory society. Memory, 30(6), 669-677.

Gudjonsson, G. H. (1997a). The members of the BFMS, the accusers and their siblings. The Psychologist, 10(4), 111-115.

Gudjonsson, G. H. (1997b). Accusations by adults of childhood sexual abuse: A survey of the members of the British False Memory Society (BFMS). Applied Cognitive Psychology, 11(1), 3-18.

Gudjonsson, G. H. (1997c). Members of the British False Memory Society: The legal consequences of the accusations for the families. Journal of Forensic Psychiatry, 8(2), 348–356. http://doi.org/10.1080/09585189708412016

Howe, M. L & Knott, L. M, Conway, Martin. A (2018) Memory and Miscarriages of Justice. Routledge.

Maran, M. (2010). My Lie: A True Story of False Memory. Jossey Bath.

Patihis, L., Ho, L. Y., Tingen, I. W., Lilienfeld, S. O., & Loftus, E. F. (2014). Are the "memory wars over"? A scientist-practitioner gap in beliefs about repressed memory. Psychological Science, 25(2), 519–530. http://doi.org/10.1177/0956797613510718

Patihis, L., and Pendergrast, M. (2019). Reports of recovered memories of abuse in therapy in a large age-representative U.S national sample: Therapy type and decade comparisons. Clinical

Psychological Science, 7(1), 3–21. http://doi.org/10.1177/2167702618773315

Otgaar, H., Howe, M. L., Patihis, L., Merckelbach, H., Lynn, S. J., Lilienfeld, S. O., & Loftus, E. F. (2019). The Return of the Repressed: The Persistent and Problematic Claims of Long-Forgotten Trauma. Perspectives on Psychological Science, 14(6), 1072–1095. https://doi.org/10.1177/0956797623510718

Otgaar, H., Howe, M. L., Dodier, O., Lilienfeld, S. O., Loftus, E. F., Lynn, S. J., ... & Patihis, L. (2021). Belief in unconscious repressed memory persists. Perspectives on Psychological Science, 16(2), 454-460.

Pendergrast, M. (2017). Memory Warp: How the Myth of Repressed Memory Arose and Refuses to Die. Upper Access Books.

Sexual Offences Act (2003). Legislation of the United Kingdom government.
https://www.legislation.gov.uk/ukpga/2003/42/contents

Shaw, J., Leonte, M., Ball, G & Felstead, K. (2017, May 28-31). When is the issue of false memory raised in historical child sex abuse allegations? An archival study of 496 British cases. Paper Presentation. European Association of Psychology and Law, Mechelen, Belgium.

Shaw, J., & Vredeveldt, A. (2019). The recovered memory debate continues in Europe: Evidence from the United Kingdom, the Netherlands, France, and Germany. Clinical Psychological Science, 7(1), 27-28.

CONCLUSION

By Henry Otgaar

How psychological trauma can affect people's lives has captivated the interest of scholars for many years. A major plank surrounding this topic is the question of how psychological trauma is recollected. Although a wealth of research has revealed that traumatic experiences are well remembered, misconceptions concerning traumatic memories abound (e.g., McNally, 2005; Wagenaar & Groeneweg, 1995). One particular misconception concerning traumatic memories is at the foreground of the current book. That is, in this book, the idea that traumatic memories are unconsciously repressed in pristine form is elaborately explained and the harm that this idea carries is described as well.

The controversial nature of repressed memory can be seen in several ways. First, the idea that traumatic memories can be unconsciously repressed does not square with research showing that traumatic memories are well remembered.

However, what is true is that people who have experienced trauma often do not want to talk or think about the trauma and sometimes even want to forget the trauma. These coping strategies are a far stretch from repressed memory (e.g., Otgaar et al., 2019). Second, repressed memory is sometimes confused with plausible memory processes such as ordinary forgetting or a lack of encoding (McNally, 2005). More importantly, the idea of repressed memory is not in line with the philosophy of science in which theoretical concepts should be able to be falsified. Specifically, the idea of repressed memory cannot be tested or falsified for the simple reason that the memory is inaccessible and cannot be reached. The only way to test its concept is when the memory is recovered but then the memory is not repressed anymore. Taken together, the idea of repressed memory rests on shaky scientific grounds.

In this book, it becomes evident that the topic of repressed memory can exert damaging consequences in legal, clinical, and academic contexts. In clinical and legal contexts, therapists believing in repressed memory can suggest to their patients that current symptomatology are the result of hidden memories of abuse. Such suggestive interventions can inadvertently lead to the recovery of memories which are actually false memories of abuse. Such false memories can lead to false accusations and even in worst cases, wrongful convictions. But also in academic contexts, the topic of repressed memory is problematic (Battista et al., 2023). That is, the topic of repressed memory is for example linked with the memory disorder dissociative amnesia. Because this disorder is listed in diagnostic mental health manuals such as the DSM-5, it has the allure of a scientific concept while in fact it is as similar and problematic as repressed memory (Mangiulli et al., 2022).

To conclude, it has been argued that the topic of repressed

memory and dissociative amnesia is akin to discussing alleged alien abductions and UFOs or the new term Unidentified Aerial Phenomena (UAP) (Otgaar et al., 2023). The National Aeronautics and Space Administration programme (NASA) is studying these UAPs in a scientific way. What NASA first does is to investigate whether UAPs can be explained in a plausible scientific way such as that they reflect weather balloons or airplanes. When they fail to find plausible explanations, this does not immediately mean that UAPs are from outer space. What is often the case is that there is a lack of data to confidently explain these UAPs.

This is the same as what occurs with cases of alleged repressed memory and dissociative amnesia. Instead of resorting to "alien" origins of memory loss (e.g., psychological trauma), many – if not most – of these cases can be explained by using scientific concepts. In the end, science is the answer to these difficult and challenging cases as to make sure to prevent miscarriages of justice from happening and to support real victims of trauma.

Professor, Dr Henry Otgaar, is a research professor at the Leuven Institute of Criminology and Professor of Legal Psychology at Maastricht University.

References:

Battista, F., Mangiulli, I., Patihis, L., Dodier, O., Curci, A., Lanciano, T., & Otgaar, H. (2023). A scientometric and descriptive review on the debate about repressed memories and traumatic forgetting. Journal of Anxiety Disorders, 10273

Mangiulli, I., Otgaar, H., Jelicic, M., & Merckelbach, H. (2022). A critical review of case studies on dissociative amnesia. Clinical

Psychological Science, 10(2), 191-211

McNally, R. J. (2005). Debunking myths about trauma and memory. The Canadian Journal of Psychiatry, 50(13), 817-822

Otgaar, H., Howe, M. L., Patihis, L., Merckelbach, H., Lynn, S. J., Lilienfeld, S. O., & Loftus, E. F. (2019). The return of the repressed: The persistent and problematic claims of long-forgotten trauma. Perspectives on Psychological Science, 14(6), 1072-1095.

Otgaar, H., Howe, M.L., Patihis, L., Mangiulli, I., Dodier, O., Huntjens, R., Krackow, E., Jelicic, M., & Lynn, S.J. (2023). Repressed memory and dissociative amnesia: The unidentified aerial phenomenon of memory loss. Manuscript submitted for publication.

AFTERWORD

By Michael Naughton

The urgent need to move from 'believe the victim' to 'question the allegation': Why language matters.

Language matters. It matters because the words or phrases that we use reflect how we think about social and legal issues and what we do, or don't do, or what we consent to be done in our name, in response to them, whether that be as individuals or as a society.

The phrase 'believe the victim,' which relates to allegations of rape, child sexual abuse (CSA) or sexual offences more generally, is particularly problematic. It can, and does, lead to a false allegation and/or wrongful conviction and/or imprisonment of innocent victims who don't seem to matter. Indeed, the rationale of 'believe the victim' is concerned only with obtaining convictions against sexual offenders; with increasing the statistics on convictions for sexual offences. In the rush to this end, proponents of the 'believe the victim' mentality show a blindness and total moral indifference to the extensive range of harms caused to innocent victims of false allegations and of alleged sexual offences, their families and society, because those falsely accused and wrongly convicted are done in our name.

In consequence, such innocent victims can be conceptualised as mere collateral damage in an ideological war that has no interest in the truthfulness of such allegations, nor with whether justice is achieved, either in terms of the correct and rightful conviction of an alleged sex offender or the acquittal of an innocent victim of a false allegation and the bringing to justice of the individual making the false allegation.

The roots of 'believe the victim' can be traced to the Jimmy Savile Affair, which represented a key moment in the history of alleged child sexual abuse specifically, and alleged sexual offences, generally, in terms of the inversion of the presumption of innocence for those accused of sexual offences.

Knighted for his charity work, somewhere in the region of 500 posthumous allegations of sexual abuse were made against the former DJ, television personality and hitherto 'national treasure' in 2012, which prompted a moral panic in society that exists to this present day about predatory sex offenders escaping justice.

A major problem is that the pendulum swung too far such that innocent victims became increasingly vulnerable to false allegations and the wrongful convictions that stem from them in the clamour by those leading the enquiry into Savile to bring all sex offenders to justice at all and any cost.

The joint report by the Metropolitan Police Service and the NSPCC into the allegations of sexual abuse against Savile, for instance, was uncompromising in its approach. Entitled, *Giving Victims a Voice*, even though Savile was never formerly charged or convicted for his alleged crimes, it was clear in its conviction that the alleged victims were victims who needed to be heard:

The allegations that have been made paint a compelling picture of widespread sexual abuse by a predatory sex offender. We are therefore referring to them as 'victims' rather than 'complainants' and are not presenting the evidence they have provided as unproven allegations.

It was the fallout from the Jimmy Savile Affair, then, and the drive to bring offenders to justice, that has seen a paradigm shift in police and prosecution responses to allegations of sexual abuse and assault making it more likely that innocent victims will be falsely accused and wrongly convicted.

From a position of questioning the veracity of allegations as a safeguard to protecting potentially innocent individuals from false allegations and wrongful convictions, the default position now is to believe alleged victims; moreover, to see complainants as victims at the point of complaint, unless there is compelling evidence to the contrary.

The College of Policing, the body which sets standards and guidance for police in England and Wales, emphasised that:

When an allegation is received, police should (now) believe this account and record it as a crime.

Similarly, prosecutors are now mandated under the terms of the new Guidelines on Prosecuting Cases of Child Sexual Abuse issued in 2013 (and revised in 2017) to work on the basis that those making allegations are victims, with prosecutors instructed to:

Guard against looking for "corroboration" of the victim's account or using the lack of "corroboration" as a reason not to proceed with the case.

These changes treat alleged sexual offences differently from every other type of alleged crime, allegations of theft, burglary, or murder, for example, which require evidence to support allegations or convictions against individuals for such alleged offences. They invert the presumption of innocence and the burden of proof on the prosecution to prove its case against an accused beyond reasonable doubt. And they, therefore, undermine the legitimacy of prosecutions and convictions against alleged innocent victims of false allegations until the presumption of innocence and the burden of proof on the prosecution are restored in the area of alleged sexual offences.

It is against this background that this article calls for an urgent shift from 'believe the victim' to 'question the allegation' in response to all allegations of sexual abuse.

Crucially, to continue to use the phrase 'believe the victim,' even to critique the concept, works to strengthen the prevailing dominant discourse. This signals the urgent need for an alternative counter discourse to be constructed and employed consistently around the more appropriate and desirable notion of 'question the allegation.'

By way of a conclusion, the Oxford English Dictionary defines an 'allegation' as:

A public statement that is made without giving proof, accusing somebody of doing something that is wrong or illegal.

It defines victim as:

A person who has been attacked, injured, or killed as the result of a crime, a disease, an accident etc.

This leads to the following observations so that language used regarding alleged allegations of sexual offences from here on uses the correct terminology:

There is no place for uncorroborated allegations in the criminal justice system of a modern rule of law society with an expressed commitment to the rights of all individuals that is enshrined enacted domestic and international human rights legislation; witch hunts and arbitrary justice are supposed to be phenomenon of the long and distant past.

Working on the basis that the individual making the allegation is the victim is equally problematic as the individual accused may well be the victim of a false allegation.

False allegations of sexual offences are also criminal offences, which strengthens, further, the urgent need to question all allegations and assume nothing in the quest for truth and justice.

Dr Michael Naughton is the Founder and Director of Empowering the Innocent (ETI). He holds a Readership in Sociology and Law at the University of Bristol.

FURTHER READING

Brandon, S. et al, 'Recovered Memories of Childhood Sexual Abuse: implications for clinical practise, British Journal of Psychiatry, 172 (1998): pp. 296- 307.

British Psychological Society, Guidelines for psychologists working with clients in contexts in which issues related to recovered memories may arise, British Psychological Society (1999), Vol. 12, pp. 82- 83.

Felstead, K. and., Felstead, R., Justice for Carol. The True Story of Carol Felstead – the Creation of a Satanic myth in the United Kingdom. Create Space Independent Publishing Platform, 2014.

French, C. and Ost, J., 'Beliefs about Memory, Childhood Abuse, and Hypnosis among Clinicians, Legal Professionals, and the General Public', in Burnett, R. (ed.), Wrongful Allegations of Sexual and Child Abuse. Oxford: Oxford University Press (2016).

Josefsson, D., The Strange Case of Thomas Quick: The Swedish

Serial Killer and the Psychoanalyst Who Created Him. London: Portobello Books, (2015).

Loftus, E. and Ketcham K., The Myth of Repressed Memory: False Memories and Allegations of Sexual Abuse. New York: St. Martin's Griffin (1994).

Mair, K., Abused by Therapy: how searching for childhood trauma can damage adult lives. Matador, (2013)

Nash, R. A. and Ost, J., False and Distorted Memories. Routledge. London and New York (2017).

Ost J. and French C., 'How Misconceptions about Memory may Undermine Witness Testimony', in Radcliffe et al. In Witness Testimony in Sexual Cases. Oxford University Press. (2016), pp. 361. 374.

Ofshe R. and Watters N., Making Monsters: False Memories, Psychotherapy, and Sexual Hysteria. New York. Charles Scribner's Sons (1994).

Patihis., L., Trauma, Memory, and Law: Lectures on repressed memories, memory distortions, and trauma. Amazon KDP, second edition. (2023).

Pendergrast., M. Victims of Memory: Incest Accusations and Shattered Lives. Harper Collins (1996).

Pendergrast, M., Memory Warp: How the Myth of Repressed Memory Arose and Refuses to Die. Vermont. Upper Access Books (2017).

Smith M. and Pazder L., Michelle Remembers. London. Sphere Books (1981).

Tavis C. and Aronson E., Mistakes Were Made – but not by me. New York. Hartcourt. (2007).

Waterhouse., R., Satanic Panic – A Modern Myth. Amazon KDP (2023).

INDEX

Adult Children Accusing Parents (ACAP) 25 26
Allen, K 154
Allen, M 154
American Medical Association (AMA) 6
Anderson, C 175
Australian Psychological Society (APS) 31
Association for Psychological Science 14
Association of Child Psychotherapists (ACP) 101
Attorney General 101 104
Baddenoch, T 153
Bennett, J 10
Bass, H 3
Barden, C 65
Beech, C 154-5
Believe the victim 206
Bergwell, S 142
Bloom, C 137
Bloom, B 137
Blunkett, D 156
Bowman, T 23
Bramall, Lord 152-3
British False Memory Society (BFMS) 9-10 21-24 27 29 36-9 149-50 169 180-90 93
Buckland, R 135
Butler, G 23
Brittan, Lord L 158
British Medical Association (BMA) 89
British Psychoanalytic Council (BPC) 101
British Psychological Society (BPS) 33
Brown, D 149 151
Castlewood Treatment Centre 15
Childhood Sexual Abuse (CSA) 24
Clinic for Dissociative Studies 65
Code for Prosecutors 23
College of Policing 207

Crews, F 20
Criminal Court of Appeal 23
Criminal Compensation Authority 25
Crossley, R 10
Davies, L 3
Day, E 144
Dick, C 156
Diamond, V 93
Diagnostic and Statistical Manual of Psychiatric Disorders (DSMD) 61
dissociative identity disorder (DID) 59-60, 65, 68, 70-1, 73
Earle Howe 140
Eronson, E 11
False Memory Syndrome Foundation (FMSF) 6, 9, 17, 19, 20, 28, 43
Felstead, C 75 – 139
Felstead, D 102
Ferneyhough, C 8
Findhorn Foundation 10
Fisher, A 19
Fisher, F 89 94-9 103-119 120-21 126-7 137-8
Fowler's Syndrome 126
Fractured Families 21 41 140
Freud, S 2
General Medical Council (GMC) 46 56 99 100
Gibbs, Sir R 153
Guidelines on Memory and the Law 173
Gidden, Master 136
Giving victims a voice 207
Greenhalgh, M 37 39
Gudjonsson, G 37
Guidelines on Prosecuting Cases of Child Sexual Abuse 208
Hanley, Sir M 153
Heath, Sir E 148 153
Henriques, Sir R 156
Hill, A 146
Hippocratic Oath 11
Howe, Sir B 156
Howes, N 67
incident management log 127
Independent Office for Police Conduct (IOPC) 156
Janner, D 157

Janner, Lord G 157
Josephson, D 143
Keates, G 149
Klein, P 63
Justice for Carol 75
Lancaster, R 13
La Fontaine, J 64
Loftus, E 5 149
Maire, Katherine 58
Maran, M 4
Marshall, S 76, 81-9, 95, 128
McDonald, Lord 158
Memory Wars 20
Metropolitan Police Service (MPS) 99
McHugh, P 7
McNally, R 7 202
Michelle Remembers 61
Ministry of Justice (MoJ) 106 139
Miscarriage of Memory 21, 44, 58 140
Multiple Personality Disorder (MPD) 8, 38, 59-60, 65
Myers, C 75 -139
My Lie 4
National Aeronautics and Space Administration Programme (NASA) 203
National Crime Agency 154 156
National Organization for Women 4
Naish, P 22
Naughton 205 209
NSPCC 24
Ofshe, R 29
Operation Midland 156
Oldfield, Sir M 153
Orne, M 7
Ost, J 38
Otgaar, H 201 203
Ousley, Mr Justice 102
Puaffley, Justice 144
Parkside Hospital 109
Paterson, V 155
Patihis, L 13
Pendergrast M 1 2 8 13 18 21 181

Pope, H 7
Pre Inquest Review Hearings (PIRH)s 105-6
Primary care support service 91
Primary care trust 91
Proctor, H 154
Quick, T 143-4
Radcliffe, S 88
Rodhouse, S 156
Ritual Abuse Information Network (RAINS), 69, 71
Royal College of Psychiatrists 71
Ross, L 17
Sandusky, J 19
Save the Children 24
Savile, J 206
Satanic ritual abuse 93
Schater, D 1
scene of crime photographs 105
Scotford, R 27-8 37-8
seduction theory 12
Shaw, J 148
Sinason, V 66 93-4 101 157
Shanley P, 11
Simandl, J 63
Shipman H 94
Showalter E, 7
Simpson, P 7
Solicitor General 134-6 151
Stevenson, J 146
Storr, W 93-8 142
Sybil 60
The Courage to Heal 6, 12, 16 25
Tavistock clinic 93
Tavris, C 7 11
Thornton, P His Honour 101
The Keepers 12
Thatcher, M 157
Trauma and Abuse Group 71
UNICEF 24
Unidentified Aerial Phenomena (UAP) 203
Van der kolk, B 17

Victims of Memory 2, 8, 17
Waterhouse, R 146
Watson, T 156-7
Watters, E 29
Weiskrantz, L 34
Wilcox, F 105 130
Wired Magazine 148
Wong, W 147

Printed in Great Britain
by Amazon